Gypsies, Preachers AND Big White Bears

One Hundred Years on Country Roads

Gypsies, Preachers AND Big White Bears

One Hundred Years on Country Roads

CLAUDIA SMITH

Published by

GENERAL STORE
PUBLISHING HOUSE

1 Main Street Burnstown, Ontario, Canada K0J 1G0
Telephone (613) 432-7697 or 1-800-465-6072

ISBN 1-896182-91-7
Printed and bound in Canada

Layout and cover design by Derek McEwen

General Store Publishing House
Burnstown, Ontario, Canada

Canadian Cataloguing in Publication Data

Smith, Claudia, 1945 -
Gypsies, preachers and big white bears : one hundred years on country roads

Includes bibliographical references.
ISBN 1-896182-91-7

1. Lanark (Ont.) : County) – History
2. Rural Roads – Ontario – Lanark (County) – History.
3. Country Life – Ontario – Lanark (County). I. Title

FC3095.L37S65 1998 971.3'8203 C98-900563-1 F1059.L3S64 1998

First Printing August 1998

Cover photo: *Marie, a young gypsy woman camped along the roadside in 1909.* PA-C21159

Introduction

This book records the activities on the country roads from pioneer days to the early days of cars. It celebrates rural life by chronicling the traffic and travellers who formed the colourful ribbon of commerce and society that wound through the countryside over the years.

The research material was ten years in the gathering. Chance comments about gypsies put me on the trail of Lanark County's colourful history. I interviewed many senior citizens who shared their memories with me and to whom I am most grateful. Their recollections of stories, handed down from long ago, made scenes of life in the forests, fields, log houses and cow byres flicker and form in my mind's eye. I have also scoured old diaries, scrapbooks, letters, newspapers and township records. Being affiliated with the Middleville and District Museum as a volunteer gave me access to many papers and photograph albums and a vast collection of Ontario statute books.

For A. J. Mckay
who shared his stories of days long passed
as well as his love of history.

"And felt the hillside thronged by souls unseen . . ."
John Masefield

Table of Contents

CHAPTER 1
Breaking Trail

FORESTS, dark and impenetrable, covered the rocky hills and fertile stretches of Lanark County before white settlers came to begin new lives in a new land. The shadowed depths under virgin pines, oaks and maples were threaded only by a few well-worn Indian trails.

When the pioneers arrived, they had to hack rough, two-tracked paths through the dense forests. Many, many hard years passed before the country folk could travel on smooth roads and look out over cultivated fields. The action and drama on the roads during the years of development provide a window into the history of the land.

In the British Isles of the early 1800s, employment was at a premium. There was an urgent need for places of settlement for the penniless workers displaced by the Industrial Revolution. Many soldiers were destitute and unemployed as well, due to the lull in the Napoleonic War and the end of the War of 1812 with the United States. The impoverished people had few choices and starvation drove the people out of their native land. In Lanarkshire, Scotland, at the Christmas season of 1819, ". . . in parish after parish, Scotsmen's families could not attend their kirk for want of clothing."[1] Plans for the settlement of Eastern Ontario moved on the wings of this desperation.

Great numbers of the discharged soldiers as well as mechanics, labourers, and weavers accepted offers of free passage, land grants, rations and implements from their government to begin new lives. Scottish Settler Societies also aided in the emigration of many poverty stricken people. Given this opportunity, the settlers had a chance to become independent. Through their own industry and courage they could make a fresh start, free of grasping landlords and relentless tax gatherers. Thousands of society settlers took the challenge and braved the rugged sea voyage in the full rigged sailing ships of the early 19th century. The trip was one of crowded discomfort, hunger and desperate illness. Many perished at sea. Cholera, dysentery and "chincough" or whooping cough took a severe toll before the ships reached the ports of Quebec City or Montreal.

Those who survived the voyage across the Atlantic struggled with flagging energies to move their possessions and families into small boats to travel up the St. Lawrence River toward Upper Canada. The immigrants helped pull the boats up savage rapids and slept in the open each night of the trip. They had to stay on guard constantly against being robbed or overcharged for any services that their guides offered.

During the early years of the 1820s, large groups of Scottish and Irish travellers arrived in Prescott. From there, arrangements were made with ox drovers or teamsters with hardy horses to transport their families and their few worldly goods. For many, their destinations were the newly opened townships of The District of Bathurst, which later became Lanark County.

There was a rough track laid out from Prescott to Perth and the history of the highways and byways of Lanark County began when these settlers made their way through the wilderness. People, young and old, who were used to the city streets and country roads of their homeland, arrived in a wild and unsettled land. Could they ever have imagined such an inhospitable place? James Gilmour, a Scottish immigrant of 1820 wrote to his brother back in Glasgow simply stating, "The want of roads is the greatest evil."[2]

Another newcomer, Andrew Bell, penned this report home, "We were three days on our journey between Prescott and Perth ... We thought the land would be covered with grass, and only a few trees here and there. But how great was our disappointment, when we found the ground was all covered with large trees, and not a pile of grass growing, except in beaver meadows . . .".[3]

The trails hacked through the forest were practically impassable. In a day's journey of approximately forty miles, much of the way was made over roads crosslaid with tree trunks in the many boggy and swampy places. With the size of these rough logs ranging from nine inches to two feet in diameter, the road surface was very uneven.

These famous corduroy roads were named for their "resemblance to the hard-wearing ridged cloth. [Their] only merit was that a cart could get across the swamp on it, but if the driver went too quickly his vehicle threatened to fall apart from the terrible jolting or his horses' hoofs might be trapped between timbers."[4]

The miserable "crosslayed" causeways of 1823 were described by British traveller, Edward Talbot, in this wry way:

> As these logs are neither square nor are they flattened, and not always perfectly straight, they frequently lie so far apart, that horses, cows, and oxen are continually in danger of breaking their limbs in passing over. Cattle of all kinds in this country are so accustomed thus to dance upon beech and maple, that, before they attain their second year, they acquire such proficiency in the art of log-walking, that I should not be at all surprised to hear of a . . . horse or bull becoming a rope-dancer.[5]

The journey overland began after the women and children were weighed as baggage and ensconced with the crates and cases on the sturdy carts. Riding in a horse drawn wagon or oxcart piled high with travelling trunks, barrels and boxes of household goods was an uncomfortable way to travel on such roads, however it was much preferable to tramping the long, long miles to the new settlements with young children held by the hand or carried on tired backs.

William Miller, who settled with his family in Dalhousie Township, arranged wagon transportation and wrote of the journey to Lanark. "Such horses for running I never saw in my life . . . I got my wife, family, and baggage, on one waggon and I thought, when we started off, that the men were mad, for they went off like a shot out of a gun, and up hill and down hill was all alike . . . [the horses] are the most mettlesome creatures I ever saw; not so heavy as yours, clean boned and lively creatures."[6]

When lurching over the rough, crosslaid logs or hitting an embedded rock, the heavily loaded carts sometimes tipped. Often settlers had arms or legs broken and young children were sometimes crushed by the heavy carts or the travelling trunks. John Climie gave this account, "The road is very rough, and they go with such fury, that sometimes, going down a hill, all is upset; however the driver is forthcoming for any damage."[7]

Many tribulations along the forest tracks lengthened the weary immigrants' travelling time to the primitive, new settlements. Mired horses, lame oxen, vast mud holes, fierce storms, losing the way and sudden illness all slowed the progress and necessitated many uncomfortable nights of sleeping in tents or rough shelters of tree boughs, in the mosquito infested forests. There was little shelter from wind, rain or the heavy dews, that descended with the darkness. As the immigrants made their way to their chosen settlements, they were appalled by the snakes they saw, by the vast clay bogs and by the dark forest with its close, stagnant air.

With no choice in the matter, the newcomers bravely squared their shoulders and kept going day after day. Often a musician in the group played old country fiddle music to lift their flagging spirits and put a light in their eyes to persevere. To the haunting melodies of highland glens, the settlers put one foot ahead of the other to press onward, as they traipsed beside the wagons.

The screech of the axles of oxcarts accompanied the settlers like the sound of wild, foreign birds. When the wooden wheel hubs got dry and hot with long use, they squeaked loudly and could be heard for miles through the forest. They even occasionally caught on fire! Liberal amounts of tallow, castor oil or boiled beaver oil were slathered on to keep them lubricated, cool and quiet.

The families arrived in the newly established villages of Perth, which had some stone buildings under construction, or Lanark, which was merely an assortment of log shanties, tents or wigwams covered with cedar boughs. The women and children settled in as best they could, while the men set out to find and appraise the lots which they had drawn from a hat. Tramping distances of up to twenty or thirty miles further up country, the men followed vague trails winding through tangled undergrowth, fallen trees, swamplands and unbridged rivers and streams. Dalhousie settler, John Climie, explained to his brother and sister in Scotland that there was "no other thing to guide [them], than a spale off the side of the trees, and if not properly attended to, [they] were sure to wander"[8] as they searched for their lots.

"Walking the blazes" or watching for the spales slashed on the sides of trees was the only way to travel to the drawn lots in the earliest days of settlement. Hardworking, rugged British survey crews had tramped through the tractless forest surveying the land. They chopped three notches in the bark of the trees along the concession lines to mark the way. Pioneers followed these blazes as best they could, seldom with the help of guides. When they reached their land grants, they found wooden posts or stone columns planted at the lot corners. Occasionally, liquor bottles stuck upside down in a pile of stones marked the corners, lending the nick name the "bottle boys" to the surveyors. No matter what marked the lots, the settlers were glad to find the markers and to know they had reached their new homesteads.

Alexander Watt, a young, single man who made his way on the rough trails of the new land in 1820, expressed his experience in Gaelic sprinkled poetry,

> The bush keeps tearing at my claes
> And still I look out for the blaze.
> All weary, wet of snow and trees
> But no home for me.
>
> I often fall and often rise
> While stumbling o'er the fallen trees,
> The snow it is above my knees
> But no home for me.[9]

The men who had left their families in the rough settlements, made their way back to pick up their waiting wives and children and then set off once again into the wilderness to take up the strands of a new life. What a daunting prospect it must have been for the settlers with young children. Some of the difficulties overcome by Dalhousie pioneer woman, Mrs. John McLelland, as she tramped through thick bush included crossing two rivers on rafts with one child in her arms and a stone of meal on her back.

Another courageous woman slogged along a bush trail towards her new home with a heavy burden of two small children on her back. In her nearly exhausted state, she suddenly realized that her load seemed lighter. Horrified to discover one child missing, she anxiously retraced her steps, staggering with panic. Her long skirts, heavy with mire, caught in the brush as she ran. Her missing young one was found sitting in a mud hole in the track, contentedly playing in the muck. She swept up the little fellow with tears of relief and warm smiles and that child grew up in the new land known by the nickname, "Spogan Dubh" (Blackpaws). [10]

After finding their way to their lots, the settlers chose a spot near a stream or creek for a reliable supply of water. They proceeded to chop down trees and those of about eighteen inches in diameter were used for building their houses. There were long, hard weeks of chopping to clear only a small clearing in which to build their log dwellings. The first house was a crude shelter, not only because of the time factor but also it was thought that when the land was cleared a more advantageous house site might be discovered. Bone weary, the families moved their few possessions from cedar

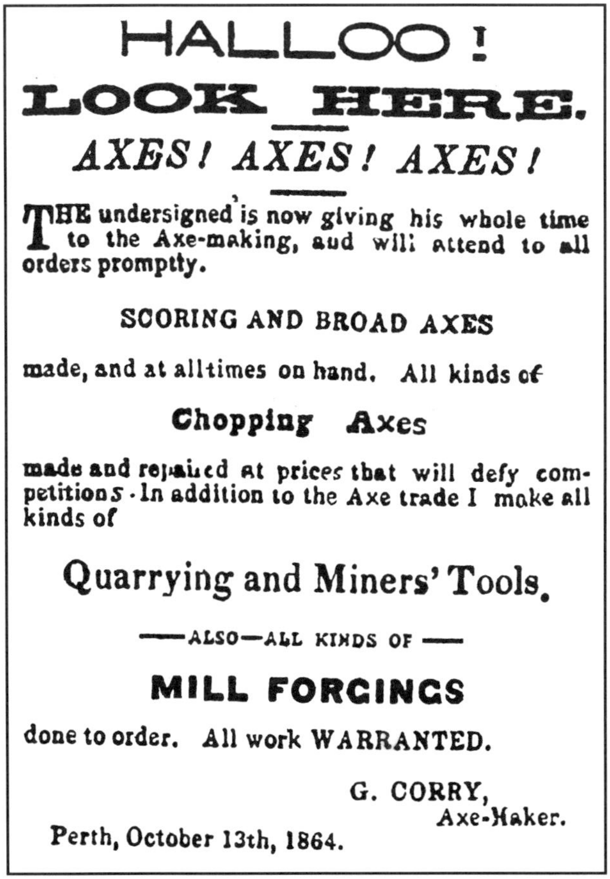
HALLOO!

LOOK HERE.

AXES! AXES! AXES!

THE undersigned is now giving his whole time to the Axe-making, aud will attend to all orders promptly.

SCORING AND BROAD AXES

made, and at alltimes on hand. All kinds of

Chopping Axes

made and repaired at prices that will defy competitions. In addition to the Axe trade I make all kinds of

Quarrying and Miners' Tools.

—ALSO—ALL KINDS OF —

MILL FORCINGS

done to order. All work WARRANTED.

G. CORRY,
Axe-Maker.

Perth, October 13th, 1864.

The settlers thought that the axes brought from Scotland were "for little use here." Local axe makers had a ready market for their strong tools that met the demands of the immigrants. *PERTH COURIER,* 1864

brush lean-tos into their small, rough houses. The floor was often sand or tamped earth. Rugs of wild animal skins were laid down and a stump near the cabin often served as a table. Glass was a scarce commodity so windows cut in the logs to let in some light were few. Uncovered windows let in hordes of voracious black flies and mosquitoes.

Once the newcomers were settled in a very rudimentary way, they looked up and outward. Friends, family and shipboard acquaintances from the Atlantic crossing were on the neighbouring parcels of ground. So besides the rough bush roads that linked tiny settlements, many pioneer trails wound through the forest to neighbours' friendly clearings and to the nearest small, log kirk or church buildings.

The crooked footpaths through the forest were often marked with stones placed on stumps as sign posts. People knew they were on the right track to a neighbour's if they followed the stones through the dense bush. Stones on stones were used as sign posts by two families of children long ago. Their forest paths converged on the way to the new log schoolhouse and they usually walked together. If one group reached the meeting place first and decided to go ahead, they put a small stone on a big stone, to indicate they had passed by. One day a mischievous fellow decided to fool the children and put a stone in the accustomed spot. Both families of children raced all the way to school thinking the others were ahead of them and that the teacher would punish them for tardiness.

The trees were so dense and tall that no sun reached through to the small clearings. In the short days of winter, the sun hardly rose out of the forest. Pioneer families had one aim after basic survival and that was to remove the forest and replace it with fields to grow crops. To hear the forest crashing to the ground to provide yet a wider bit of sky was the goal. The men tramped the forest tracks, each with an axe on his shoulder to help the other at work parties. Bees were essential for clearing the land, as familes alone could not manage the enormous job of cutting the huge trees on their land.

The women got together, when the logging bees "swarmed," to prepare food for the hungry men. So during the long day of work, both sexes had a chance to share practical ideas and give each other encouragement in the hard times of settling in a new land. However, many homesteads were a long way from neighbouring farms. After being surrounded by kith and kin in village life in Scotland or Ireland, the women on these distant tracts suffered from extreme loneliness. Their men had some contact with other men at the mill, a sawing or at a tavern but it was not unheard of for women to die of the isolation and extreme hardship of their pioneering life.

Despite the rough, exhausting bush life and the torment of the blackflies and mosquitoes, the hard working, determined families soon made progress and sent letters back to Scotland praising the land where their "free hearths stand." A Scottish emigrant wrote, "I am very well pleased to handle the axe, instead of the shuttle, and would not, for a great deal, give up my present for my past employment . . . I am relieved from taxation, rent and crushing ill-paid work . . .". [11]

Strong, well-muscled oxen worked patiently with the men. On James Waddell Senior's farm in Ramsay Township an ox was even hitched with a horse to plough the fields or work in the forest. In the 1840s, stout pairs

Oxen were mighty beasts of burden used in opening up the forested tracts and ploughing the fields.
COURTESY OF THE MIDDLEVILLE AND DISTRICT MUSEUM

How to Make an Ox-Yoke.

The ease and effectiveness with which oxen work depends largely upon the shape of the yoke. For good-sized oxen—those weighing 1,500 lbs.—the timber for the yoke should be 6 feet long and 12 inches in diameter. The toughest elm of crooked grain is the best material, as it combines lightness, strength, and durability. One side of the log is hewn smooth and becomes the top of the yoke. Upon this draw your lines—one lengthwise through the center, a second crossing this at right angles at its middle, and one 18 inches

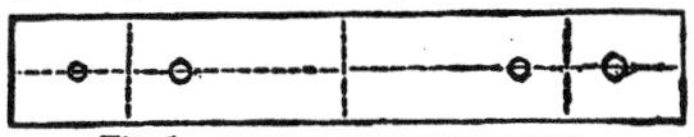

Fig. 1.—Center and cross lines.

from each end, as shown in figure 1. The outline of the yoke when finished, looking from above, is shown in figure 2; upon this the dimensions are given in detail. The holes for the bows should be two inches in diameter, bored exactly perpendicular, and one foot apart. In boring these holes, see that the log is perfectly level and secured from turning in any way. After the stick

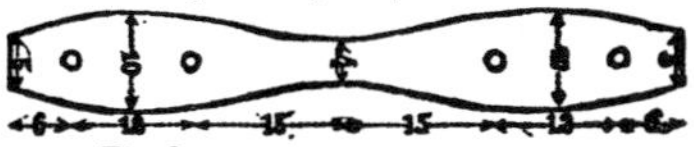

Fig. 2.—Outline of top of yoke.

has been brought into the shape shown in figure 2, next shape the upper and under sides as shown in figure 3. One half of the yoke, giving the measurements for cutting, is shown in fig. 4. The dotted line, *A,B*, is drawn 3 inches from the top. A line, marked 1, is drawn down midway between the sides of the bow, the line 2 is one inch nearer the

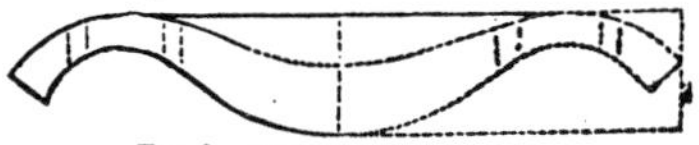

Fig. 3.—Side view of yoke.

end, and the line 3 one-half inch the other side of line 1. One foot of a pair of dividers is placed at 1, and the other describes the curve for the under side of the "hollow." Move the foot to the point 2, and describe the curve from the top of the yoke to the end, on the upper side. The curve for the under side of the end is made with the foot of the dividers placed at point 3. With these lines described, there will be no trouble in

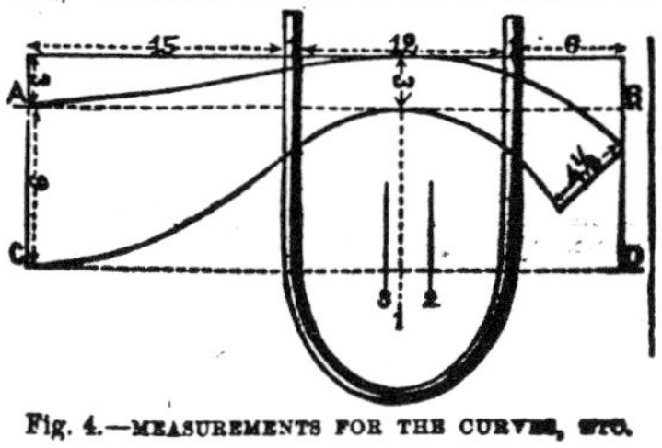

Fig. 4.—Measurements for the curves, etc.

finishing the yoke in proper shape. If the wood is green, it is best to give it all the grease or oil it will absorb; heat, and grease again. This will prevent it from cracking badly.

Instructions for making an ox-yoke from the *American Agriculturalist* magazine, March, 1881.

of oxen drew home-made sleds "innocent of iron" to town to pick up supplies. A trip of four miles took an hour at ox speed. Steered by a twelve-foot-long stick called a gad, the oxen also ploughed through the deep snows of maple bushes in the spring, steadily pulling sleds loaded with wooden sap troughs.

However, they were not always cooperative in their daily round of work in the farming partnership. Some teams learned to bring their heads together when they were working so that their yoke slipped from the back of their necks and hung below their chins. This gave the drover a great deal of trouble because he would have to stop ploughing or stumping, take out the bow pins, pull out the bows and replace the yoke in the proper position. Oxen also occasionally got into the habit of crowding and pushing each other when they worked. Their energy was wasted and when they played at such games it cut down on their efficiency.

As the land was cleared, the development of communities and commerce depended on a system of passable roads. By 1825, the population of Lanark County was tallied at 7,928 souls and communities began to offer services. Logs were hauled to the nearest pit saw or sawmill, grain was carried to mills and cow hides were taken to tanneries. Strong backs and determination were needed for transporting loads along the rutted tracks.

A sampling of the early commerce was recorded in George Easton's 1831 diary. "This day driving ashes to Conroy's leecher for melting" into potash and ". . . at Lanark, bought 20 pounds of iron for a fireplace crane." The iron was purchased from a local blacksmith who made hinges, latches and catches as well as numerous farm implements and strong cranes for swinging cooking pots over the fire.

With heavy bags of grain or flour, an iron potash kettle or a plough on their backs, the homesteaders walked long, rough miles to and from distant towns. To make the job easier, one man dragged a bag of flour fifteen miles on a deer skin which slipped smoothly over the snow. Another fellow "man-packed" two one-hundred- pound bags of salt to his farm and put them down only to cross over fences.

Oliver Caldwell, an early settler in Darling Township, produced three bags of grain from his land. He went to the bush and cut two trees which had limbs with crooks in them. He fashioned curved sleigh runners and made a jumper sled. With his grain sacks piled on his low, homemade sleigh, he started walking the many miles to Perth. He reached the mill by dark having led his ox through creeks, over hills and around boulders. When the grain was ground the next day, the sturdy fellow retraced his steps home to his waiting family.

This poem, harkening back to days long past, tells of the efforts involved in making the essential trails for travelling to the mills or stores.

A travelling group of men with ox carts stopped for a meal by the roadside. They may have been outfitters who transported settlers' possessions up from the front. They travelled well-equipped with tents, water barrel and cooking utensils.
COURTESY OF THE MIDDLEVILLE AND DISTRICT MUSEUM

We went on foot and horseback, but at last we made a way,
Broad enough, by careful teaming, for oxen and a sleigh,
But of surveying implements we did not need a load,
For a woman rang a cowbell while her husband blazed the road.
Two discs cut from a big round log made the first affair on wheels
And when that cart was coming, you could hear for miles the squeals;
We would run out doors to see it, 'twas a wonder, then you know
That pioneer conveyance of [so long ago.]
And when we had a grist to grind or trading we must do,
It meant a trip of fifty miles - a rough one it was too!
After three or four days absence, returning with our sacks,
We trudged the lonely homeward way, with flour upon our backs.
The children all were watching, for bread was such a treat,
They could scarcely wait with patience till the cakes were fit to eat.[12]

In 1822, a Ramsay Township man, Walter Gardner, carried a block of cherry wood the many miles to a Brockville mill. He ordered his wood turned on a lathe to make a screw for a cheese press. Many families had crude cheese presses that required rocks as a weight to press out the whey. Walter's idea for the screw mechanism was an ingenious innovation for his family's cheese production.

Great skeins of yarn spun from clouds of carded wool were occasionally taken to a local weaver. This was a time-saving luxury for women if the family could spare produce for bartering or coins for the service. In an 1831 diary, it was recounted that Jenny Easton took her yarn to a local weaver. It was quickly woven and a bulky roll of thirty yards of sturdy cloth was delivered to the Easton farm. Jenny paid the bill with the sweat of her brow, working in the weaver's field of rye.

In the early pioneer days, a neighbourhood often boasted only a single darning needle. This tiny household implement was absolutely necessary to sew new clothing and to extend the life of the meagre clothing that the settlers possessed. It was passed from one log home to another and the rule was that each homemaker could use it for one day in each three or four weeks. One day the word went out in the Fitzroy district that the community needle was lost. People gathered to search for the missing implement which had been dropped by Mrs. Dickson on her way to Squire London's grist mill. After what seemed a fruitless search, a cry went up that the needle was found. The sharp eyes of a little girl had caught the glint of the darning needle on a trodden tuft of grass along the path. There was much rejoicing as the nearest shop where the needle could be replaced was in Perth, a long sixty miles away.[13]

James McIlraith and his wife Euphemia settled in Lanark Township on the banks of the Wee Clyde River. They toiled together to make a new life. He wrote a poem that praised his wife and her efforts in getting supplies for their family.

We got along pretty well
By keeping a little steady.
When we needed provisions
My wife was always ready.

She and auntie would plod the trackless snows,
And never make a grumble
Although the ice was on their clothes
As big as a tailor's thimble.[14]

Long, arduous journeys on foot were made by constables and magistrates as they performed their legal responsibilities. In the very early days, James Bowes, as a constable and magistrate, delivered prisoners to Perth which was the county seat for the combined counties of Lanark and Renfrew. He "counted it a day's journey to travel to Perth from Douglas to attend a trial or deliver a prisoner."[15] The route he took passed through Renfrew, Burnstown, White Lake and then followed the Bellamy Road into Ramsay and along the Perth Road to his destination.

Trips to local mills involved much effort and often some adventure. A periodical, *The New Dominion Monthly* of March 1878, featured a tale about a hair-raising trip to a grist mill. An octogenarian, reminisced around a fire one night about yoking his oxen to a high wheeled cart, hoisting in two bags of grain and starting out on the seven-mile trip at dusk.

"I had to be back by daybreak; for our last dust of meal had been done up in the previous days baking." He knew the route through the bush well, as did his faithful cattle, but as they proceeded he noticed his oxen "were becoming uneasy and excited, casting anxious and nervous glances all around them and switching their tails uneasily." Wolves were yipping and growling, and came out of the forest running ever closer to the beasts. Hurrying the oxen was out of the question because they were not on a road but in rough, unbroken bush where the way had to be picked with caution.

Within three miles of the mill a wolf jumped at one oxen's neck. Both animals began to run and other wolves leaped on their backs. The farmer was flung to the floor of the cart and "the poor oxen, wild with terror and fleeing like the wind, kept up a continuous and unearthly roar, their tails curled over their backs and their eyes darting out of their sockets."

As they neared the mill, the wolves faded into the forest one by one. The miller helped the shaken man and his poor beasts. Then with lantern in hand, he walked back into the woods to find the grist that had slipped out of the cart. He also accompanied the fellow home when the grain was ground. The two oxen recovered but had to be killed because their nerves were completely shattered and they could never be worked with comfort or pleasure again.

Young Willie Croft was walking home one dark night along a rutted, stony track. Suddenly, the quiet darkness was split by the unearthly, piercing scream of a lynx close at hand. In a cold sweat, the fellow picked up a rock for scant protection from the creature and made his way home. The next morning he found the heft of the rock was such that someone had to help him carry it out of the kitchen.

A bear in Dalhousie gave Isabella McNicol a bad fright. She went out one morning with her small son, William, to join her husband in the bush where he was chopping trees. She left the child sleeping in a maple sap trough while she went to a nearby creek for some water.

When she turned back she saw a bear heading for the sap trough. Dropping her bucket, she ran bravely toward the bear, screaming an alarm to her husband. Between them they frightened the beast back into the forest.[16]

As late as 1864, there were newly arrived immigrants braving the wild back country. They tramped the trails, looking for a good place to make a home. William Morris trudged through "fear muddy roads" from Darling Township to Arnprior and Pakenham and then finally settled in Rosetta. He later chronicled his journey with these remarks. "I had travelled so much for a place to make a home I was beginning to wish I had never crossed the deep. Why had I left the home where my fathers sleep. I sighed for Scotland's shore."

In spite of the stones, forests and cold, people kept coming across the Atlantic searching for a better life and the message that reached back across the waves to families in the homeland was, "You need not be afraid to come here; it is easier for a poor man to get into a good way of living, than in Scotland."[17]

> Early one winter, a stout hearted Scotsman arrived and built a log shanty. He was determined to have a good chimney built in the spring. All winter he fretted whether "there wad be stanes eneuch on his lot to build a chumla." The neighbours assured him there would be stones enough. As the snows melted back the heads of Lanark boulders appeared. The old man was in high spirits and exclaimed, "Aw'm guan to get stanes eneuch to build my chumla!" When spring arrived he realized there were stones enough to build a cathedral.
> *Rose Belford's Canadian Monthly and National Review*, February, 1882.

---

1 Charlotte Whitton, *A Hundred Years A-Fellin'*, 1842-1924, (Gillies Brothers, Limited, Braeside, Ontario, 1943), p.10.

2 Robert Lamond, *A Narrative of the Rise and Progress of Emigration from the Counties of Lanark and Renfrew to the New Settlements of Upper Canada;* (Glasgow, 1821), Canadian Heritage Publications, 1978; p.99.

3 Ibid., p.73.

4 Edwin C. Guillet, *The Story of Canadian Roads*; (University of Toronto Press, 1966), p.59.

5 Edward Allen Talbot, *Five Years in the Canadas including a Tour of the United States of America in the Year 1823*; (Longman, Hurst, Rees, Orme, Brown and Green, London, 1824), p.150.

6 Lamond, *A Narrative*, p.80.

7 Ibid., p.90.

8 Ibid., p.91.

9 John M. Collins, *The McIntosh Family of Lanark County*, (Ontario, Second Edition, 1991), Poem by Alexander Watt, *Cold, Cold Day To Me*, p.A2-2.

10 Edwin C. Guillet & Jessie E. McEwen, *Finding New Homes In Canada*, (Thomas Nelson & Sons Ltd. 1938), p.101.

11 Lamond, *A Narrative*, p.104.

12 Jean Rankin, Scrapbook, Courtesy of the Middleville and District Museum; Anonymous Poem, Sixty Years Ago.

13 Edna G.Lowry, *A Family Record of Pioneer Scottish Families in Lanark County and Their Descendents*, p.123.

14 Penny McIlraith, *A McIlraith History, Descendents of James McIlraith 1789-1881*, (Toronto: Ontario, Canada,1985), p.76.

15 Lowry, *A Family Record*, p. 56.

16 *McNicol Family History*, Courtesy of the Middleville and District Museum.

17 Lamond, A Narrarive, p.76.

CHAPTER 2

Over the River and Through the Woods

ROAD BUILDING advice in the pioneer days of Lanark County was simple; "If you keep the stones out and water off, you have a road." However this was far easier said than done. The rutted tracks that linked the embryo communities presented problems of major proportions for the travelling public. For decades after the first settlers arrived, ox carts, hay wagons and family buggies jolted over rocks and low stumps. Rainy weather always compounded the difficulties of travelling, turning the roads into a sea of mud. The "first oots," as the first generation out from the old country was called, bore the brunt of getting the roads into passable shape.

In the early days of settlement, the concessions were surveyed and marked off, but did not have roads along them. They had to be built as the settlers took up their lots. Many roads did not follow the concession lines because large rock outcroppings, vast swampy areas or steep hills made travel difficult for humans and their beasts of burden. The early roads wound through the countryside, meandering like quiet streams and the settlers walked or drove these ribbons through the forest to get to mill or market.

Work on the early township roads was done by mandatory statute labour. Before taxation covered the costs of road work, the farmers built and maintained the roads and bridges. Designated portions of the roads were the responsibility of township appointed overseers of highways, later called pathmasters. Each was responsible for keeping the roads of his jurisdiction in good repair with the statute labour of his neighbours. Under the direction of the pathmaster the men worked on the roads in the vicinity of their own property lines using their own oxen and later their own teams of horses.

George Easton, of Dalhousie Township, wrote about his civic duty in his diary as early as 1837. "June 30: . . . finished my time on the roads. 4 days labour."

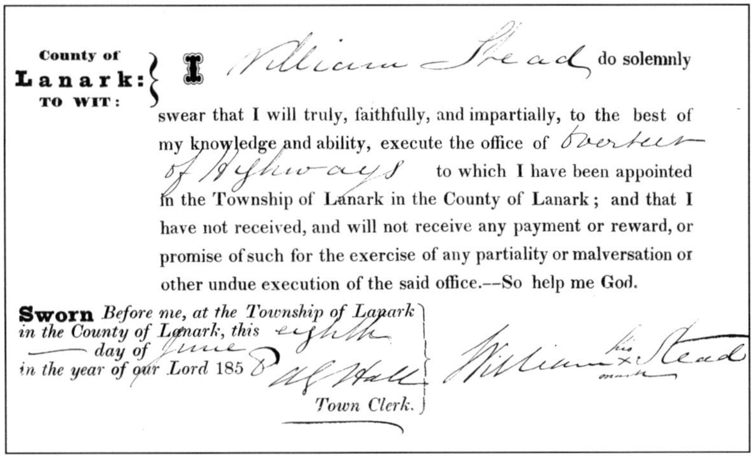
County of Lanark: TO WIT: } I William Stead do solemnly swear that I will truly, faithfully, and impartially, to the best of my knowledge and ability, execute the office of Overseer of Highways to which I have been appointed in the Township of Lanark in the County of Lanark; and that I have not received, and will not receive any payment or reward, or promise of such for the exercise of any partiality or malversation or other undue execution of the said office.—So help me God.

Sworn *Before me, at the Township of Lanark in the County of Lanark, this* eighth *day of* June *in the year of our Lord* 1858 }

A. Hall *Town Clerk.*

William his x mark Stead

The sworn pledge by William Stead with "his own mark" that he would impartially carry out the duties of overseer of highways. 1858 LANARK TOWNSHIP RECORDS

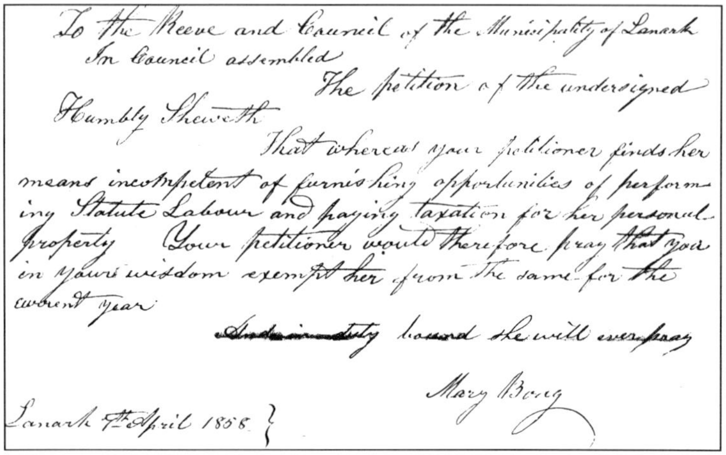
To the Reeve and Council of the Municipality of Lanark In Council assembled

The petition of the undersigned Humbly Sheweth

That whereas your petitioner finds her means incompetent of furnishing opportunities of performing Statute Labour and paying taxation for her personal property Your petitioner would therefore pray that you in yours wisdom exempt her from the same for the current year

And in duty bound she will ever pray

Mary Borg

Lanark 7th April 1858

A petition to the Lanark Township Council from a widow for exemption from her statute labour obligations for the year 1858.

Every man from the age of twenty-one to sixty was liable for two days of statute labour on the roads of their township. Landowners were required to work on the roads for a certain number of days according to the assessment of their property. Widows often asked for special dispensation to get a neighbour to take on their statute labour obligations or to be excused from it. The 1855 *Municipal Manual for Upper Canada* set the number of days labour owed, in correlation to property values at this rate:

- two days' labour for less than £50 assessment;
- three days' labour for £50 to £100 assessment;
- four days' labour for £100 to £150 assessment, and so on.

General road work was hard labour but removing the stumps of the huge pine and maple trees that were cut to clear the roads was the worst job of all. Sometimes district magistrates sentenced drunks or other disorderly folks to the tough work of stumping. The pine stumps made durable and efficient fences when they were pulled out and laid on their sides with the roots fanned out.

The early roads had twists and curves in them, but topographical features were not the only reason that they did not always take the shortest route between two points. James McIlraith and his family settled at "The Clachan," on the Wee Clyde River, in 1820. They worked at clearing their homestead long before there were any roads in the area at all. Many years later, a road building gang was heading toward their farm. Clachan Jimmie, as James was called, knew the law set out in an Ontario statute that stated that new roads could not "encroach upon any building or pass through any pleasure ground, garden, yard or orchard."[1] Not wanting to lose a single foot of his cleared land to the road, he planned to outwit them. He spent the night before the road workers reached his property planting potatoes. Thus the road was forced to curve around his garden. He later wrote a small verse about the episode:

Auld Clachan Jimmie
Canny as twa'
Planted his taties
And laughed at them a'.[2]

The upkeep of the network of roads linking the small villages and towns was a major concern for the municipal councils. Petitions were continually made to the councillors for improvements on different concession lines and bridges. In 1853, a council was petitioned about a section of road where, during the previous spring, summer and fall, ". . . people riding on horseback were necessitated to alight on passing [parts of it] and people passing with carts, waggons or other vehicles of any descriptions were necessitated to have their axes by them to make such temporary repairs as were essential for the present and no more...".[3]

The raging forest fires of 1870 forced Peter Stewart to petition the reeve and councillors of Lanark Township for help. He wrote, "On account of the great fires last summer a great deal of the sixth concession line was burned down and blocked up with fallen trees and intirely stopped, your petitioner would therefore pray for all the statute labour in his house, I think it will be about 12 days, to be expended in that part of the line."

This scene of men at statute labour "is not a caricature: it is a simple holding of the mirror up to nature," according to the original caption. Sometimes, if the work was interrupted, the road was left bumpy with piles of earth which remained unspread for the whole season.
AMERICAN AGRICULTURALIST, NOVEMBER, 1881

A group of workers on the village roads of Middleville. Circa 1900. COURTESY OF THE MIDDLEVILLE AND DISTRICT MUSEUM

Difficulties and conflict arose over surveys when changes were necessary to fence lines. The township councils had to deal with complaints from their pathmasters as well as those from the farmers. A petition from pathmaster Charles Stewart, in 1871, showed that he was put to a great deal of trouble while performing his duty because of a deliberate falsehood told by a farmer as to his line fences. Mr. Stewart told the councillors, "He accosted me on the road . . . he charged me with his scythe and was going to let the heart's blood out of me and latterly he drove me away with a handspoke and swore he would have my life if i ever came back to warn him again. thus i am threatened with prosecution on the one hand and assassination on the other. as i am unwilling to submit to either i hearby appeal to you as your servant for protection and direction in the execution of my duty . . ."

Some pioneers lived with great inconvenience on their roads. Samuel Stevenson and his family had "for twenty-four years been labouring under a great disadvantage on account of a precipice on the concession line which [they] must travel in going to either mill or market." It was impossible to get around this impediment without encroaching on private property which also took them far out of their way. In 1871, he wrote to Municipal Council of the United Townships of Lanark and Darling that he had endeavoured to fight "his way as best he might without complaining on account of the general poverty of the country. But now when a general improvement has taken place and the whole country has undergone such a vast change for the better your petitioner thinks it hard that he should in his old age still labour under such a discouraging disadvantage." The councillors

Statute labour gang working on the road with the tools of the day, a road scraper, rakes and shovels. Circa 1900. PA-72-9250

took his case into favourable consideration and arrangements were made that allowed the family's passage to and fro without trespassing.

Bridges were especially hazardous parts of the road system everywhere. The inspectors of schools in different counties had first hand experience with high water and weak bridges as they travelled to their far flung school sections. In 1871, it was reported that some repairs were absolutely necessary because a school inspector had had to swim his horse over the Madawaska River in four places.

To protect bridges and to save unnecessary draws on tax monies for repairs, as well as for public safety, a Lanark Township bylaw was passed in 1865 "that any parties driving sawlogs or square or sided timber, neglecting to place glancing booms previous to attempting to drive such material through any bridges . . . shall be liable to a penalty of not less than $10 and not more than $50 for each breach." In spite of such laws, glancing booms were often not put in place by the logging companies that used the rivers as highways for their timber.

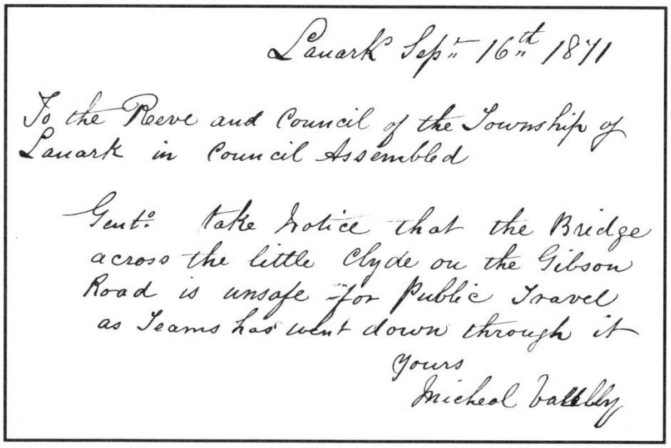

Lanark Sepr 16th 1871

To the Reeve and Council of the Township of Lanark in Council Assembled

Gent. take Notice that the Bridge across the little Clyde on the Gibson Road is unsafe for Public Travel as Teams has went down through it

Yours

Micheal [illegible]

An 1871 complaint about the safety of a bridge across the Little Clyde River. LANARK TOWNSHIP RECORDS

In 1871, plea for just such bridge repairs came from J.W. Anderson, whose petition "humbly shewed that . . . the bridge on the crossroad between lots 20 and 21 on the fourth concession of Lanark Township, has in consequence of a jam of lumber passing through between the piers thereof been damaged so as to render it impassable for a team." He was especially anxious to have the council oblige in providing money or labour to fix the bridge because he ran a busy sawmill on the River Clyde and needed the bridge for his customers' trade and for delivering the barrels, sawn lumber, shingles and chairs produced at the mill.

> Besides pathmasters, other coveted municipal jobs included appointed poundkeepers who cared for stray animals, fenceviewers who arbitrated between neighbours with disagreements about fence lines, livestock evaluators who investigated animals killed or maimed by wildlife, inspectors of licences and road surveyors.

The settlers were inconvenienced by the lack of a bridge across the river at the narrows between Clayton and Taylor Lakes for years. Before a mill was built at Bellamy's Mills (Clayton) in 1825, the crossing had been nearly all a dry swamp. Then the mill dam inundated the area upstream. A family named Bennett lived near the narrows and operated a ferry across the water for a few years. Later it was crossed by planks and then three hewn logs chained together. In 1858, farmers petitioned the Lanark Township Council for a bridge across the river that was "indispensably necessary for the convenience of the country, generally being several miles shorter by that route to the Catholic church in Ferguson's Falls, to Perth and to the railroad depot at Almonte."

Timber was cut, planks sawn and thick pegs driven deep into the wood of the stringers for a new bridge of an innovative design by the contractor James Sullivan. It floated! In August 1859, James Foley, William Hogg and John McCoy, the three commissioners in charge of the project, proclaimed the bridge finished. They reported, "At present horses and oxen with any carts, waggons, buggyies or carriages of all descriptions loaded or unloaded may pass safely and securely without impediments."[4]

The public was grateful to see the enormous quantity of timber and labour that was used for such a small financial outlay in the bridge contract with Sullivan. The narrows where the bridge was built had only been "the abode of black snakes, muskrats, water fowl and other wild animals. Now it was daily resorted to by the human species and on Sundays and holidays, more than one hundred people met at the bridge to see the curiosity and construction of the mammoth floating bridge."[5] People marvelled at the new bridge and commented on how the hardships were fast disappearing since the years when the "first oots" had arrived.

Eighteen years later in 1877, wheels, wind and waves had taken their toll on the bridge. A contract was let to Timothy Sullivan to build a new bridge on top of the old one as it had become impossible for horses to travel on it. The old arch over the waterway and the fifty-foot passing portion in the centre of the structure were to be kept as they were in the old bridge. Seasoned oak and elm pins fastened the stringers together and the bark was taken off every piece of the top covering where the planks touched each other. A stout railing was bolted along each side of the bridge.

Countless horses and wagons, farm machines, funeral processions and people on foot, as well as cows, sows and sheep travelled over the log bridge, which caught the wind like a mast in stormy weather and rocked on the waves. In high water, the logs tended to pile up and teams had to climb up the logs. Summertime brought low water and the bridge stretched down and made an easier surface for horses. In 1914, the first car bumped over the logs. It was not until 1943 that the deteriorating Floating Bridge was closed to traffic by the Ontario Municipal Board.

Long before 1900, there was also a floating road on the main route from Clayton to Carleton Place. It went straight across a sink hole in Ramsay Township. The residents' first attempts to bridge the twenty acres of muck was a corduroy swamp road. The crosslaid logs were supported on a somewhat reliable base of roots, long grasses and stumps. Whenever it got oozy, the neighbours' statute labour was used to pile on more logs. At one time the timbers of an old Presbyterian church and even the logs from several barns were piled in .

The roads department battled the sink hole for years and years. In 1910, a new

The Floating Bridge, facing north, across the narrows between Clayton and Taylor Lakes. Built in1859, it served the rural area well until it was closed in 1943. COURTESY OF THE MIDDLEVILLE AND DISTRICT MUSEUM

attempt at bridging the sink hole included crosslaying new logs and ditching the passageway. This was unwise as the roots and brush had stabilized the road bridge. By spring the road had disappeared into the ooze. An acre or two of pine was cut and laid in but once again it was gone by spring. The road did not disappear over night. It just gradually sank into the murky depths.

The next attempt was a half moon crook in the road around one end of the sink hole. Stringers and logs were pinned into place and great hope was held out for this new road-bridge. In 1927, Bert Miller's heavy threshing outfit, which included a steam engine, the thresher and a team of horses pulling a water tank, approached the bridge. Mr. Miller and his crew noticed a pocket of black spruce waving back and forth on the other side of the sink hole and while the moving trees raised comments, the warning was not heeded. The front wheels of the heavy engine were barely on the end of the bridge when suddenly the bridge began to tip sideways! The engine weight kept it from tipping completely and the crew managed to get the front wheels right up onto the bridge. After working exceedingly quickly to stabilize the back end, they got the whole outfit up onto the bridge and crossed to the opposite shore.

The remnants of the Ramsay Township floating bridge over the sink hole. Circa 1930. COURTESY OF ROBERT MILLER

The movement and weight of the machinery on the log and gravelled road approach had set up the wave motion in the thick sludge that rocked the trees and then tipped the bridge. If they had reached the bridge a half-minute earlier they would have lost the whole thing into the depths of the sink hole. That was the last heavy machinery to cross the bridge and by 1939, all efforts to bridge the sink hole were abandoned. Road engineers bowed to the power of the water and muck.

Over the years, as machinery got heavier and heavier, hearts lodged in throats as men drove their huge machines - huge in weight and investment - over the log bridges of the day. In 1908, a Fallbrook newsman for the *Perth Courier* was relieved to report that, "The traction engine belonging to W.G. Keays passed into Fallbrook over Mud Lake and Fall River bridges without any accident."

Wooden bridges were damaged by the wheels of big steam engines. Deep cleat marks were left in the planks. More than one engine operator had the county constable come in hot pursuit on a bicycle to administer a fine for bridge damage caused by his machine.

Horsedrawn steam engines and threshing mills put a strain on the roadways too as they were taken from farm to farm. Some of the

A horse and buggy crossing the lower bridge across the Mississippi River in Drummond Township near Lanark Village in the early 1900s.
PHOTOGRAPH BY M.M. KNOWLES. COURTESY OF THE LANARK AND DISTRICT MUSEUM

early mills weighed as much as 6,800 pounds. Tolls were set especially for these extremely heavy loads. Before it was lawful to run a traction engine over toll-roads the engine driver had to notify the keeper of any tollgate on the road two months previous to running.[6] Then the owners of the toll-roads were obliged to make all bridges and culverts strong enough for the safe passing of such heavy vehicles.

Water figured largely in the transportation system but not always in the form of bridges. There was a barge link from the St. Lawrence River up the Rideau Canal and into the Tay Canal to Perth. Horsedrawn barges, with the names *British Queen*, *Forwarder* and *Siren*, travelled the Tay Canal after it opened in 1834. They carried all the merchandise for Perth and outlying areas that had come from suppliers in Montreal and various towns along the St. Lawrence River commonly called "the Front."

By 1849, the Tay Canal was silted in and the locks fell into disrepair. The days of barges were over and supplies for the fast growing town were landed by ferry boat at Oliver's Ferry (now Rideau Ferry) on the Rideau River. All the teaming necessary to deliver the goods to Perth was controlled by Archibald Campbell's widow, Elizabeth. Her teamsters loaded her heavy wagons and glossy, big teams of horses hauled the merchandise to the stores in town. The reminiscences of Donald Fraser, who clerked at the general store of Murray, Morris & Company, told of boxes and barrels of goods reaching Perth via the ferry. He also reported that passengers travelling to Perth rode in leather spring stage coaches which swayed and jounced them in a lurching rhythm over the miles. Nathan Mott and Pat Spence worked for years on that stage line and their work was praised with these words "more careful and capable men never handled the ribbons."[7]

Many immigrants stayed at Cameron's stopping place near the Mississippi River as they trudged from Perth to their newly drawn lots near the settlement of Lanark. In 1821, Malcolm, the enterprising young son of the inn keeper, ferried the travellers across the expanse of the river in a dug-out canoe, a crude boat or on a raft.[8] No one was travelling with livestock in the early years so a boat was adequate for transporting people and the packs and sacks they had brought to the new land.

Gradually, travelling became easier and easier as the construction of plank, macadamized and gravelled roads was encouraged by the provincial and local governments. The 1855 *Municipal Manual For Upper Canada* granted private road companies the right to collect tolls in consideration of planking, gravelling or macadamizing a road or building a bridge. Any persons passing with horses, carts or carriages, or driving cattle, swine or sheep along the road had to pay. Road building could be organized by a minimum of five people who formed a small joint stock road company. Each company had to build a minimum of two miles of road in accordance with the enacted standards. There could only be one toll-gate every five miles and the toll could be levied on the work for no longer than twenty-one years after the work had been completed.

The municipal manual allowed for raising money by toll on any bridge or road, to defray the expense of construction and repair. In 1855, the toll charge was one penny, per mile, per horse and vehicle, with a half penny extra for every additional animal. Herds of animals driven along the road cost a half penny for every score of sheep, cattle or swine per mile. Heavy vehicles loaded with masts, spars or hewn or round timbers exceeding two tons in weight, were charged a toll of two shillings six pence. The wheels of such vehicles had to have five-inch rims to prevent the destruction of the roads.

Colonel Andrew Playfair headed a Bathurst District special road committee in 1849. The abundance of pine made the construction of plank roads connecting Lanark, Balderson, Perth and Playfairville economical. "The Old Pine Road" was made of planks cut in three-to four-foot lengths, much of it supplied by John Gillies' sawmill. For a few years, loads of lumber and other heavy goods rattled over this smooth flooring. By 1856, people were refusing

One of the five toll-gates between Lanark and Perth. Circa 1900. SUBMITTED BY ALEX BOWES TO *ALMONTE GAZETTE*, JULY 26, 1989

to pay the tolls because the pine planks had rotted away quickly and the surface resembled, in its days of disrepair, the jolting corduroy roads found elsewhere in the county.

Many roads that led to Perth in the 1870s were stoned toll-roads but in some places the ruins of the old plank road lay in plain view. The road of pine and later of stone was owned by two different joint stock road companies, one from Lanark to Balderson and the other from Balderson to Perth.[9] Both companies sold out their interests when roads became the responsibility of the county in 1904.

Montague Township was plagued by indifferent or nonexistent roads for many years. The hardworking farmers had a difficult time moving their farm produce to mills for processing or for shipment to market along the Rideau River system. The township council was repeatedly petitioned for an improvement in the roadways as they were deemed "unfit for even corpses to travel."[10]

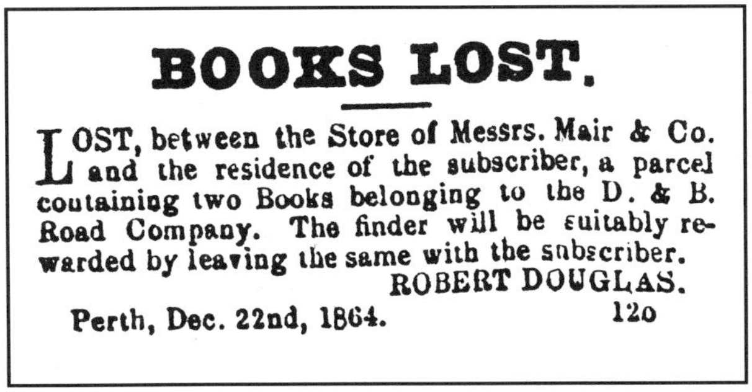
BOOKS LOST.

LOST, between the Store of Messrs. Mair & Co. and the residence of the subscriber, a parcel containing two Books belonging to the D. & B. Road Company. The finder will be suitably rewarded by leaving the same with the subscriber.
ROBERT DOUGLAS.
Perth, Dec. 22nd, 1864. 120

Four of Lanark County's toll road companies were the Lanark & Drummond, the Drummond & Bathurst, the Bathurst & Mississippi and the Scotch Line Company. This advertisement indicates a spot of trouble for the D. & B. Road Company in 1864. PERTH COURIER, JANUARY 6, 1865

The delivery of sleighloads of wood to towns often involved going through three or four tolls on the way. On bitterly cold winter mornings, the teamsters hated to have to take off their mitts to get money out of their pants' pockets at each gate to pay the toll-gate keeper. In 1858, the British currency system was changed to dollars and cents in Upper and Lower Canada. Pence and shillings or nickels and dimes, it mattered little what the coins were called on the frosty trips to town. According to the law, change did not have to be given for an amount of larger than five shillings. People had to have as close to the exact change as possible.

"A winter road is opened from Richard Healy's in Ferguson's Falls to Perth. By travelling this route all tollgates may be avoided except one on the southern edge of Lanark." *Lanark Era*, 1898.

Going to church did not cost the families any hard earned coins at the toll gates. An Ontario statute of 1877 decreed:

> *All persons going or returning from Divine Service on any Sunday or obligatory holiday in or upon and with their own carriages, horses or other beasts of draught and families and servants shall pass toll free through every turnpike or toll.*

It also allowed free passing on toll roads to:

> *Officers and Non-commissioned Officers and men of the Volunteers, being in proper staff or regimental uniform dress or undress and their horses.*

The *Municipal Manual For Upper Canada* for 1855, made it illegal to damage any lamp or lamp post placed near the side of the road by a toll house or to willfully extinguish the lamp that marked the toll-gate. It was also illegal to pull down or deface any table of tolls fixed at the check-gates or on any sign-board erected by the road company.[11] The fine was a maximum of fifty shillings plus the costs of damage repair.

Vandalism was not the only difficulty that toll-gate keepers had to contend with. Another was collecting tolls from drivers who refused to pay. If a person refused to produce the necessary coins, his horse, carriage or other beasts could be seized together with bridles, saddles, harness and other accouterments.

Gatekeepers were also at risk, as they sat alone in the toll station at night. One dark night toward midnight, a gatekeeper heard a horsedrawn rig rapidly approaching. The driver stopped a short distance from the toll-gate but then came on and paid the toll. His head was muffled up with only his eyes showing so the keeper could not note anything of his description.

As the sound of the rig died away in the night air, the gatekeeper felt his way back into the dimly lighted station. He had just entered the outer door when a masked man, who must have been let off by the driver, dashed forward and crashed down on his head with a heavy metal object. The poor man fell heavily to the floor, bleeding and unconscious.

The injured gatekeeper was helped by the next person to come along and the constable was notified. The amount of money stolen was not large, only $20 with most of it in pennies. People in the area went on the alert for someone with an unexplainable excess of coppers.

A shoemaker near Balderson allowed some local men, who decided to play detective, to meet in his shop at night since he usually pegged away at his shoe mending until late in the evening. One night, these earnest men decided that they knew who had robbed the gatekeeper. They brought the suspect to the shoemaker's shop and locked him in a back room. All the while, he shouted and protested his innocence and the shoemaker sat quietly mending his shoes.

Suddenly the voice of the accused changed to an insistent shout. At first these calls were ignored, since the constable was on his way. But then his shouts began to sink in. He said he had found a black mask and a sack of coins in a corner of the room. The men turned to grab the shoemaker, but he had bolted out the door and off into the night. He was later captured and broke stones in the jail yard for five years.[12]

A band of men awoke a Farmersville gatekeeper one night in April, 1862. They tumbled him into their sleigh and rushed into the house again. They seized his sister and put her into the sleigh as well. The two hapless victims were driven off five miles into the country and left on the road in their night clothes. Meanwhile the lawless gang emptied the toll house of all the furniture and then set the place on fire. The country folk were outraged by this attack on their faithful gatekeeper.

> **Toll House Cookies**
>
> (Perhaps sold at a toll house or given as a special treat by the lady of the place.)
>
> 1/2 cup butter, 3/4 cup granulated and brown sugar mixed, one egg, 1 1/4 cup flour,1 tsp. vanilla, 1 small tsp. soda dissolved in 1 tsp. hot water and one bar of chocolate broken into small pieces and a fistful of nutmeats. Mix and bake as cookies.
>
> *Mary Graham Archibald*

There were other activities that went on near toll houses that were simply highjinks. Duncan Ferguson and his wife Annie ran the 6th Line Bathurst & Drummond toll-gate. It stood at the intersection of Armstrongs Corners, between Lanark and Balderson. Annie collected the coins from travellers when her husband was away. Duncan's second job was levelling off the road between Balderson and Lanark. Buggy wheels worked the gravel to the sides of the road and Duncan with another man, kept the road smooth with hand rakes.

Road Notice

Notice is hereby given, that a meeting of the Shareholders of the Scotch Line Toll Road Company will be held in the Cheese Factory, Scotch Line, on SATURDAY, 17th APRIL, 1897, at the hour of Two o'clock p.m., and that tenders will be received by the undersigned for the lease of the toll gates until the evening before the meeting: and that the Treasurer will be present to receive the annual subscriptions.

P. McKINLEY,
Secretary.

Bathurst, March 29, 1897. 4ir

Classified advertisement in the *Perth Courier,* April 2, 1897.

The toll-gate was located near a stopping place and an inveterate patron of the hotel bar often wagered with passers-by, that he could balance and run on the rim of a wheel of their oxcart as fast as they could drive their oxen. So all for the price of another drink, the scene would unfold with the spry, sure-footed fellow running on the wheel rim, like a treadmill. From the top of a nearby hill, down past the toll-gate to the hotel, the antics were accompanied by shouts, cat calls and the crack of a whip as the oxen were urged on to make the acrobat lose his foothold. He earned a good number of drinks with this stunt over the years for this man was no mean athlete. It was said that he could still turn cartwheels when in his eighties. His obvious athleticism gave him an unfair advantage over the travellers, who looked at his inebriated state and figured they would get an easy drink to continue on their journey.

Good roads were expected and hoped for but were never taken for granted. In the spring of 1889, four people were travelling from Perth to Smiths Falls and their high stepping carriage horses got mired right in the middle of the highway. The horses went down to their bodies and the wheels of the carriage settled below the hubs. The passengers were forced to get out in the mud and unhitch the team. A kindly neighbour brought a chain and a fresh team and drew the carriage out backwards. The *Rideau Record* of April, 1889 reported, "The place is a disgrace as can be said for nearly every road in the [North Elmsley] township." It was little wonder people began to complain when they were paying to pass on the roads but the roads were often impassable.

Town streets were criticized as well as country ones but one sly comment in the *Perth Courier* of 1865 asked, "Whoever heard of a woman with pretty ankles and whole stockings complaining of wet sidewalks or muddy crossings?"

The road company monopolies and tolls were petty and vexatious and "people disliked them cordially." Newspaper reports of 1887 said the provincial government was "friendly to the idea of abolishing toll gates." Sound principles of settlement were to be adopted so that no builder of a road could reasonably find fault, as the monies they had invested were to be returned to them. Lanark County had an interest in freeing the road. Two townships, as well as portions of others were prepared to do it. By 1904, the last of the roads in Lanark County were freed from tolls at a cost of $19,346. Now the people could move goods and travel freely on the roads.

As early as 1891, people were also complaining publicly about having to do statute labour. It was thought to be "an antiquated concern belonging to the days of logging bees, potash making and ox yokes." Work had to be wrung out of the young men by the pathmaster and many refused and would prefer to pay a sum rather than have to do compulsory manual labour. It was a distasteful way of levying taxes for the taxpayer and the collector.[13]

By a provincial act in 1904, one-third of the cost of county road work was to be contributed by the Government of Ontario. With this financial assistance, good progress was made in the improvement and building of the county byways. Stone for the new road projects was broken by a crusher, which was purchased by the county in the spring of that year. The outfit consisted of a 17-horsepower engine, a wagon equipped with a water tank and a crusher which turned out 10 to 12 cords of stone per day. A rotary screen attachment with bins and chutes received the stone and carried it to special dump wagons for hauling to the road bed.

The county road gangs lived in a camp in order to stay close to remote job sites. The camp, comprised of half a dozen tents for the horses and the men, was moved from time to time to points along the work. The usual wages for labour were $1.23 per day plus board, while a man with a team earned $2.50 per day.

As settlement progressed, the countryside was much tamed and the trees were cut back everywhere. An 1873 Ontario statute enabled municipalities to pass a bylaw allowing "*any person who shall plant any fruit trees or any trees . . . for affording shade on any highway within the municipality, an abatement of statute labour or out of a general fund a sum of not less than 25¢ for every tree planted.*"

Statute labour was still in force in many townships into the 1930s. Since there were no paved roads, the pathmaster's job included hauling and spreading gravel. Men with horse drawn graders continually graded the gravel from the edges of the road back to the centre. Cutting the brush and tall roadside weeds was also the responsibility of the road gangs. Some help with roadside maintenance came from road herds. Cattle and sometimes horses were allowed to forage as best they could on their own. These animals grazed the road edges nipping off branches, weeds and grass.

> An 1841 bylaw in Ramsay Township set a fine of one shilling per head for all cattle trespassing within a quarter-mile of mills, stores, taverns or churches on preaching Sundays. There was also a shilling fine for a yoke of oxen at large without a bell.

In days gone by, road crews and local people did not call the roads and familiar terrain by their concession and lot numbers. The names of the crossroads, low places, hills and road bends had special meanings that reflected the history of the land.

Centres of commerce were often indicated by place names. Factory Corners was the location of a cheese factory. Tannery Hill, Mica Hill, Potash Hill, Marble Bluff, Shanty Hill, Coal Pit Hill and Iron Road whispered of past industries. Milling operations gave their names to side roads and settlements. Foley's Mill which became Hall's Mills on the Indian River; Herron's Mills on the Clyde; Bellamy's Mills now Clayton on the Indian River; and Shipman's Mills, now Almonte on the Mississippi River are cases in point. Flower Station and Lavant Station are two of many places whose names bear witness to the route of the Kingston and Pembroke Railway that once chugged up from Kingston. Whisky Town was a centre of a different sort of commerce.

The Old Ferry Road led to the banks of a river where supplies were landed at a ferry crossing. Oliver's Ferry Road or First Rapids Road once bore the weight of oxcarts loaded with potash and crops on the way to markets along the Rideau River and on to Montreal. A route travelled by a farmer collecting milk from his neighbours to deliver to a nearby cheese factory was called the Milk Wagon Road.

Prominent landmarks, trees and plants were frequently used to indicate specific spots. Creek Road, Basswood Corner, Sugarbush Hill, Hickory Hill, Pine Grove, Tansy Hill, Maple Creek, Blueberry Point and Appletree Falls, now Appleton, are a few. Grapevine Hill was an exceptionally winding section of road in the Flower Station area. MacDonald's Corners was often referred to as The Hill because the approach to the village was up-hill from every direction.

Animals got into the name game with places like Porcupine Mountain, Fish Creek, Wolf Grove, Cuckoo Nest Road, Beaver Dam Bridge, Skunk Street and a crossroads in Beckwith Township called Skunk's Misery. The Sow's Belly was the name given to a runway across a road from one heavily wooded area to another. It was frequently used by she-bears or sows and their cubs.

Fiddler's Hill is a long, steep slope where exhausted Scottish settlers are said to have reached a state of desperate discouragement. They had nearly given up their trek to their drawn lots in the Watson's Corners area when the bold-spirited fiddle music of one of their countrymen gave them new heart and resolve to complete their journey.

A lengthy hill near Tatlock gave teamster's a chance to roll a cigarette and enjoy a smoke without holding the lines as their horses leaned into their collars and pulled their loads up the hill. Thus this part of the road was called the Long Hill. Another mountainous road was called the Whip-on because sometimes the whip was used to encourage the efforts of teams hauling heavy loads up the steep grade.

Landscape also took on the names of residents. Examples are the Indian Road, Indian River, Polly's Hill, Ellis's Hill, Biddy's Creek, where a small girl loved to play, Givens' Corners, The French Line, O'Connor's Spring, Paddy's Bridge, Shane's Common, Granny White's Hill, Hand's Settlement and the Moulton Settlement. Dobbie's Flats was long known as an old corduroy road. Even the presence of periodic residents was recorded in the name The Gypsy Field Gate. Gypsies often pulled into the field to camp for the night as they passed in their never-ending travels. People credited Satan with the responsibility for more than one sharp turn in the countryside because there are several places with the descriptive name, the Devil's Elbow.

The Corduroy Road reminded users of the old type of roads that were once built and Thunder Bridge got its name because the slab covering on it rumbled like thunder when wagons or Model T Fords went over it at any speed. Children delighted in the Tickle Belly Hills, a section of road that lifted the stomachs of passengers as cars went over the crests of three rolling hills. The Section House Road name speaks of the days when sections of railway lines were the responsibility of section men and the railroad provided houses for their families. The Sessions Road was named after the forerunner of township councils that met four times a year. School Hill and the Wee School Hill speak for themselves.

The story of the people and the roads is mirrored in all these names. The landscape of past generations comes alive on road signs today where the history has been carried forward.

---

1 *The Municipal Manual for Upper Canada*, Fifth Edition, 1855, p.281.
2 Penny McIlraith, *A McIlraith History, Decendents of James McIlraith 1789-1881*, (Toronto: Ontario, Canada, 1985), p.73.
3 Lanark Township Records, Petition, many signateurs, 1853.
4 Lanark Township Records, Commissioner's Report, 1859.
5 Ibid.
6 *The Revised Statutes Of Ontario*, Volume 2. 1877, p.1949.
7 *The Perth Courier*, January 29, 1919.
8 Howard Morton Brown, *Lanark Legacy Nineteenth Century Glimpses of An Ontario County*, (The Corporation Of The County of Lanark, 1984), p.106.
9 C.M.Forbes, History of Lanark Covering an Eighty Five Year Period, *The Perth Courier*, January, 1906.
10 Howard Morton Brown, *Lanark Legacy, Nineteenth Century Glimpses of an Ontario County*, The Corporation of the County of Lanark, 1984, p.121.
11 *The Municipal Manual For Upper Canada*, 1885, p.298.
12 Dee MacEnne, (Donald McNicol), From a scrapbook, Courtesy of the Watson's Corners Library.
13 *The Almonte Gazette*, November, 1891.

CHAPTER 3

Entrepreneurs and Rogues of the Road

THE SETTLERS came to Lanark County with little except expectations for a better way of life. Having fled unemployment, extreme poverty and famine, many had no ready cash on hand. They grubbed potatoes and some grain from the soil between the tree stumps. With wildlife for the shooting, sugar from the maple trees and tea brewed from maidenhair ferns, pine needles or dried raspberry leaves, they eked a meagre living out of their clearings. Relatives back in Scotland were encouraged to take a chance on the new land with wise words like, "A strong family is better than a good purse." In 1821, a letter from H.L. to his family in Glasgow declared, "There is another happy circumstance, - the clergy are not a dead weight here upon property. They have lands assigned to themselves, and they have no claim on the other landholders, neither tithe nor tiend."[1]

The only cash the settlers and their families earned came from selling barrels of potash. Hardwood trees cleared from their land were burned in a sheltered spot and the ashes were put through a wooden leecher. The resulting "lees," or liquid from the saturated ashes, was boiled in a potash kettle until it was red hot and thick. Then it was ladled into iron coolers to harden and put into barrels. Great care was taken with the loads of potash as they were drawn by oxcart to Perth or other centres for export to Montreal. Potash, being concentrated lye, was very corrosive and drovers knew that a splashed drop of water and potash took the hair right off an ox's back.

Barrels of potash, weighing up to seven hundred pounds, were transported on square timber rafts to Montreal or Brockville for shipment to England. This potash was a valuable commodity used in the manufacture of dye, glass, soap and for bleaching cloth. Selling potash was a bonus for pioneering families. It gave them some ready cash in an economy that was based primarily on the barter system. It was not until the 1870s, when cheese factories opened to buy milk, that people finally had a regular source of income that could be counted on.

The settlers travelled to villages to get staples such as salt, sugar, tea and sometimes flour and cloth. All the other necessities of life were grown on their increasingly productive farmlands. Bartering homegrown goods for the essentials was a common practice. The barter system provided the store keepers with eggs, wool, potatoes and other farm produce to sell to townspeople. Grain was an important item of barter in stores and the many distilleries provided ready markets for any extra grain.

This excerpt from a poem tells of the difficulties the homesteaders had when dealing with merchants:

> To Perth or on to Brockville, we went to find a store,
> As there was no competition, the wily merchant seized
> The golden opportunity to charge what price he pleased-
> I've sometimes paid five shillings for a pound of common tea
> And the price of muscavado [sugar] was often one and three.[2]

To keep their shelves filled with dry goods, the storekeepers travelled to Montreal twice a year. All classes of goods were displayed at a large "purchasing market." Merchandise was selected for the season and shipped to stores in the spring and fall. The new fashions as well as the latest gadgets for home and farm use were stocked on the shelves and in the bins of the stores.

The increasing population and the steady expansion of settled land brought a need for newspapers. The *Bathurst Courier* kept the citizens informed as early as 1840. The popular ones, in the 1870s, were the *Carleton Place Herald*, the *Perth Courier* and the *Toronto Globe*. They were sold in the stores in towns as well as by mail subscription. People in town for supplies picked up newspapers for themselves and their neighbours.

J.R. Gemmill started a small newspaper, in Lanark, in 1850, called the *Observer*. It had twenty-four columns of reading matter including poetry. John McEwen travelled about the countryside on horseback selling subscriptions. He was part of a staff of agents and collectors tending to the business of selling this modest paper from Perth to Admaston. The *Observer* had influence and power in Eastern Ontario at the time.

The need for more outside goods grew as the population increased and this niche was filled by commercial travellers who first appeared in the towns and villages of Lanark County in the 1860s. They were salesmen who displayed their wares in hotel showrooms or in halls where merchants could view their merchandise and place orders for their shops. The travellers expanded their territory from "the Front" along the St. Lawrence River northwards and they saved the merchants the arduous and costly trips to Montreal.

As the years passed, more and more commercial travellers offered their services so by 1873, local councils in Ontario began to license transient traders who occupied premises in a locality for temporary periods. This extra revenue for the townships was a welcome addition to perennially low coffers.

Advertisements recruiting commercial travellers appeared in local newspapers:

Wanted:

Active man of good character to deliver and collect in Ontario for an old, established manufacturing wholesale house based in Chicago. $900.00 a year, sure pay. Honesty more than experience required. 1900

Newspaper advertisements of 1900 indicate how anxious the hotels were to offer their services to these travelling salesmen:

The Victoria House (Hotel)
of Lanark
is large and comfortable,
centrally located in the village,
well furnished throughout,
having fine sample rooms
for Commercial Travellers;
with large yards and
abundant stabling;
headquarters for the
Hopetown, Middleville, and
Watson's Corners Stages.

•••

Clyde Hotel
Lanark, Ontario
Jas. Dobbie, Prop.
Large commodious and
well furnished bedrooms.
First Class Sample Rooms.
One of the largest and best
Hotels in the County.
Prices moderate.
Large Stable Accommodations.

The Clyde Hotel in the early days of its history. Mr. Thomas Dobbie, the proprietor of the hotel when this picture was taken, was born in Lanark County in 1828.
COURTESY OF THE LANARK AND DISTRICT MUSEUM

Advertisements of new stage routes were important to road-weary travelling salesmen. In 1871, this notice was welcome news.

Travellers to Clayton
should bear in mind
that a stage runs daily
between Almonte and Clayton.
The fare is only 50 cents.
Will be a great convenience
to Commercial Travellers
who heretofore had to
hire their own conveyance.

Commercial travellers made the local news.

"A Commercial traveller was snowed in at Clayton from Thursday to Monday"
Almonte Gazette February, 1888.

" Mr. James McDonald, Commercial Traveller, paid Hopetown a visit on Wednesday." *Lanark Era*, April 6, 1898.

Travelling salesmen were offered insurance in *Munsey's Magazine* of 1902. Their life was eventful as they covered the long miles by wagon or on foot and accidents frequently put them out of commission.

As the forests were felled and the countryside opened up, the roadways became ribbons of commerce and communication. Fields grew from small patches where the pioneers felt fortunate to "gee and lap furrow around a goodly number of stumps," to larger tilled fields where the ploughmen could be proud of their long straight furrows. Cultivation of the land in Lanark County

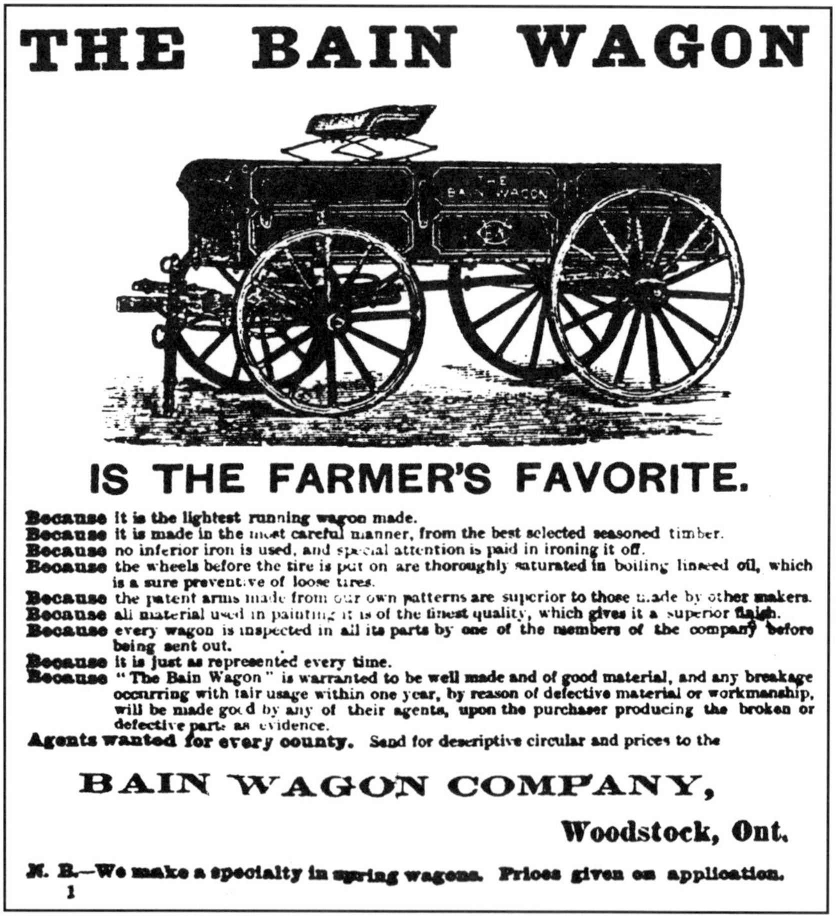

A Bain Wagon advertisement of 1883 in the *Farmer's Advocate* magazine. These highly prized wagons were also sold through the Massey-Harris agents in the late 1800s.

always included a surfeit of "ground knots" or rocks, however, with the trees chopped down, sunlight could reach the gardens. The field crops grew well and the pastures held thriving cattle, sheep and horses.

A new type of travelling salesperson appeared on the winding roads of the expanding settlements, doing business directly with the homesteaders and bypassing the merchants in the stores. These transient traders were called hawkers. They visited villages and farm houses representing companies who sold tea, organs, jewelry and other small items and agricultural implements. Often they took orders for goods that were delivered later.

Agents were sought by the Bain Wagon Company of Woodstock, Ontario. Their farm wagon was a favourite due to its light weight, fine construction and good warranty. The representatives of this product had a solid future because of the company's reputation for quality and they were welcomed by the farming communities.

The Daly Tea Company of Napanee, Ontario had sales representatives throughout Lanark County. With closed-in wagons drawn by sleek teams of commercial horses, the salesmen travelled the country roads taking orders from the farming folk for a year's supply of green tea. Wooden chests lined with lead and covered with colourful, flowered paper filled the tea wagons. The heavy wagons had brakes that were applied with the pull of a lever to ease the job of the horses as they headed down a steep hill to a village or along a back road. The sand and grit on the wheels screeched when this brake was snapped on and announced the arrival of the tea man in hilly districts.

By 1909, the Salada Tea Company was a stiff competitor of the tea pedlars. They advertised in the *Perth Courier*,

> The finest leaves of Ceylon tea plantations...
> Packed in lead packets
> to preserve the delicious flavour and aroma.
> Sold only by grocers,
> Never by pedlars or in bulk.

Locally-based hawkers travelled from Lanark Village each winter. A.G. Dobbie ran the lucrative Clyde Foundry in Lanark. His foundry manufactured stoves, sewing machines, ploughs and tinware. During the winter months of the 1870s, the pedlars of the firm travelled far and wide with their merchandise piled on

A Daly Tea Company tea chest up for auction. They were covered with colourful, flowered paper and lined with lead to keep the tea fresh. CLAUDIA SMITH

sleighs. The foundry's popular stove, the "Fire-King," was found in many kitchens in the counties of Lanark and Renfrew.

Reed organ salesmen travelled from farm to farm in the late 1800s. They sold their musical instruments for one hundred dollars each. Music was an important part of the home amusement scene at this time because other entertainments were few and far between. Families gathered around the organ of an evening or with visiting neighbours and enjoyed music and singing. The salesmen did a brisk trade in the countryside, even selling organs to the occasional school section for the school house. Young women with musical talents snapped the reins on their horses' backs and made their way to homes around the countryside to teach young people about the vagaries of the pedals and buttons of the new organs. It was considered a suitable occupation for young ladies of the time.

Later, pianos too were peddled from the back of wagons. A wily piano salesman, who travelled the roads with a piano on his wagon, stopped in at farms and told the families that he was having an axle problem or that a wheel was

Robert Anderson, the original cultivator of the Lanark Greening apple, with a relative Katie Lindsay, 1913.
COURTESY OF ALMA ANDERSON

loose. He explained that he must unload the instrument while he fixed the wagon and that he had to get the piano in out of the weather. He never once had to reload a piano after the family saw it in their house or heard a daughter play some music. Other pianos, ordered through the Eaton's catalogue, were delivered to the nearest railway depot. These precious purchases were bundled in horse blankets to cushion the trip along the rutted roads in the back of the excited family's farm wagon.

Dust was raised on the roads in the late 1800s and early 1900s by Robert and John Anderson of Fallbrook. These local fruit tree salesmen delivered saplings around the countryside in the spring. They peddled the rootstock for their newly developed apple, the Lanark Greening, from the back of a wagon. This new apple was a fine, hard cooking apple and "a good keeper." To this day, Lanark Greening apple trees can be found in orchards or gardens near abandoned farm buildings or next to the stone foundation of a log house long fallen through time.

The Andersons delivered orders of young cherry, plum and pear whips, as well as the yellow and red varieties of the Sheep Snout apple, which were valued by farming families for winter use. In the fall, they peddled barrels and bushel baskets of pungent smelling apples from one farm gate to the next.

People trusted local salesmen more than strangers. "Buyer Beware" was an important lesson. Many farm families learned it the hard way when they responded to smooth talk and lavish promises and reached into their pockets to make cash payments for unseen purchases.

In the summer of 1869, a sleek, silver-tongued fruit tree salesman travelled the roads. This hawker with his luscious looking plates of beautiful, rosy fruit, victimized the farmers to the extent of $3,000. This was the first appearance of such salesmen in the area and the honest yeomen were easily convinced to sign for large orders of nursery stock. A consignment of dry twigs was delivered to the yard of the Victoria Hotel at Lanark. Some individuals had bought thirty dollars' worth but years afterward, only an occasional Siberian Crab tree was the result of this expenditure of money and labour.

In 1900, a daring fakir, under the guise of an eye doctor, was travelling the length and breadth of Lanark County. A public service warning in the *Lanark Era* stated, "He is dark, with a clean shaven face and is accompanied by a youth with fair hair. He goes to a house, examines the eyes and tells you that you have cancer at the back of the eye or some such thing, and if you neglect getting glasses you will lose your sight. So he sells you a pair of glasses at anywhere from $3.00 to $12.00."

Business must have been good for the eyeglass hawkers because in 1909, their presence in the area was again publicized and people were alerted that the impostors charged a high price for eyeglasses and customers would soon find that the goods were badly misrepresented. If they looked for the man to complain to, he was no longer in the area. Dealing with local opticians was highly recommended.

There were many scams and schemes presented by enterprising rogues. This headline in the *Lanark Era* in April, 1900 warned farmers about travelling salesmen in Ontario who were not as honest as the sun.

Fakirs Whose Business is Swindling Farmers
Sign No Papers For Them

The paper gave details about an unsuspecting man who, trying to be cooperative, supposed he was signing a testimonial for cattle feed. He found out not long after to his dismay, that the paper was instead an order for $180 worth of the product.

Other rogues, posing as cattle buyers, stayed for several days at different farms, always with free board, on the strength of the

NUMBER 1720

SHARES

Ottawa & St. Lawrence Electric Railway Company

INCORPORATED UNDER SPECIAL ACT OF THE LEGISLATURE OF THE PROVINCE OF ONTARIO

CAPITAL STOCK $5,000,000

SHARES $100.00 EACH.

This Certifies that Clara Adelaide Croft — is the owner of One Shares of the Capital Stock of

Ottawa & St. Lawrence Electric Railway Company

transferable only on the books of the Corporation by the holder hereof in person or by Attorney upon surrender of this Certificate properly endorsed.

In Witness Whereof, the said Corporation has caused this Certificate to be signed by its duly authorized officers, and to be sealed with the Seal of the Corporation this Sixteenth day of February A.D. 1915.

President. Secretary.

An Ottawa & St. Lawrence Electric Railway Company share purchased by Clara Croft in 1915 for $100.00.

COURTESY OF THE MIDDLEVILLE AND DISTRICT MUSEUM

purchases they were supposed to make. No purchases were made and the men lived free as they travelled the roads.

In 1869, another agricultural swindle involved a smooth talking canvasser selling subscriptions for a new, patent land roller. A man called Richards said the roller would be cheaper if more people ordered, so he obligingly agreed to take $10 promissory notes to be applied to the price when the machines were delivered. The salesman with his pockets filled with notes and no doubt a smirk on his face, left the county and promptly sold the notes to a Mr. St. John. This fellow immediately proceeded to collect the face value of the notes from the farmers and they were compelled to pay up. As much as two to three hundred dollars was taken from communities who could ill afford to lose such sums. Once again many struggling homesteaders were left poorer but wiser.

A brawny, dark haired fakir, travelled the roads of Lanark in 1896. He introduced a cunning, little article intended to prevent the waste of oil and wicks in coal oil lamps. For the privilege of placing a piece of wire gauze over the end of a wick, he charged twenty cents per lamp. He claimed that the device would prevent the burning of the wick and the smoking of the chimney. The money was handed over by many prominent citizens but the gauze burned off in two nights, after the traveller was on the road again.

Appearing on doorsteps in many villages, with a tale of a neighbour's reduced circumstances, came an aptly named Mr. Good. He fleeced honest citizens of their coins ranging from 25¢ to $5 in the spring of 1909. The *Perth Courier* reported, "He said he had started a fund for his unfortunate neighbour who had an outbreak of hoof and mouth disease in his herd of cattle. He was accompanied by his dutiful wife who wore a sincere expression as if she had left the cows at home and was in fear she should not return home in time to milk them before dark. Trudging through the snow from door to door, the artful dodgers made a touching scene and the shekels rolled. Thus the innocent world was deceived as they passed out of town with words of thanks." The pair went on with their "good work" in many villages of the county.

Promises of an electric railway belt line from Ottawa to several outlying counties were in the air around 1915. Some clever and persuasive entrepreneurs held public meetings in Middleville, Lanark, Balderson, Perth, Smiths Falls, Athens, Toledo and the Frankville vicinities. They sold subscriptions for stock in the Ottawa - St. Lawrence Electric Railway Company. Visions of the prosperity such a transportation link would bring made excitement run high. Hotel keepers boarded the salesmen without charge. Local people lost working days in their fields driving them around looking for more clients. Others cut cedar trees for railway ties. All were given shares in lieu of payment.

Shares for $100 each were bought by many citizens. Local papers skeptically warned, "there was such a volume of smoke belching ..." from the authorities surrounding the proposed electric railway, that readers were asked "to beware, lest there be a fire." Enough looseness was in evidence to warrant close scrutiny of the entire promotion. Great concern about endangering the money of the public was expressed because the enterprise seemed doomed by another competing railway system. Indeed the scheme failed by an order of the Ontario Legislature which halted franchise extensions to any private companies.[3] The smooth talking promoters left the investors with little more than worthless pieces of paper and some useful experience in investing.

News in the *Rideau Record* newspaper of 1899 warned of an infestation of robbers north of Lanark County. These villains robbed milk houses and held up travellers in lonely places by the wayside. The gang numbered about twenty and people were frightened to travel the roads alone. Another instance of highway robbery involved a fourteen-year-old boy who was overtaken by two scoundrels in a sleigh. He was ordered to remove his boots. He handed them over and had to tramp the rest of the way to school in his stocking feet.

Pakenham was once the scene of a grisly murder when an old man refused to sell his prized team of horses to a passing traveller. The fellow came back at night, killed the farmer and stole his horses, sleigh and buffalo robes. He drove to Burritt's Rapids in his ill-gotten sleigh but when he tried to sell the whole outfit there

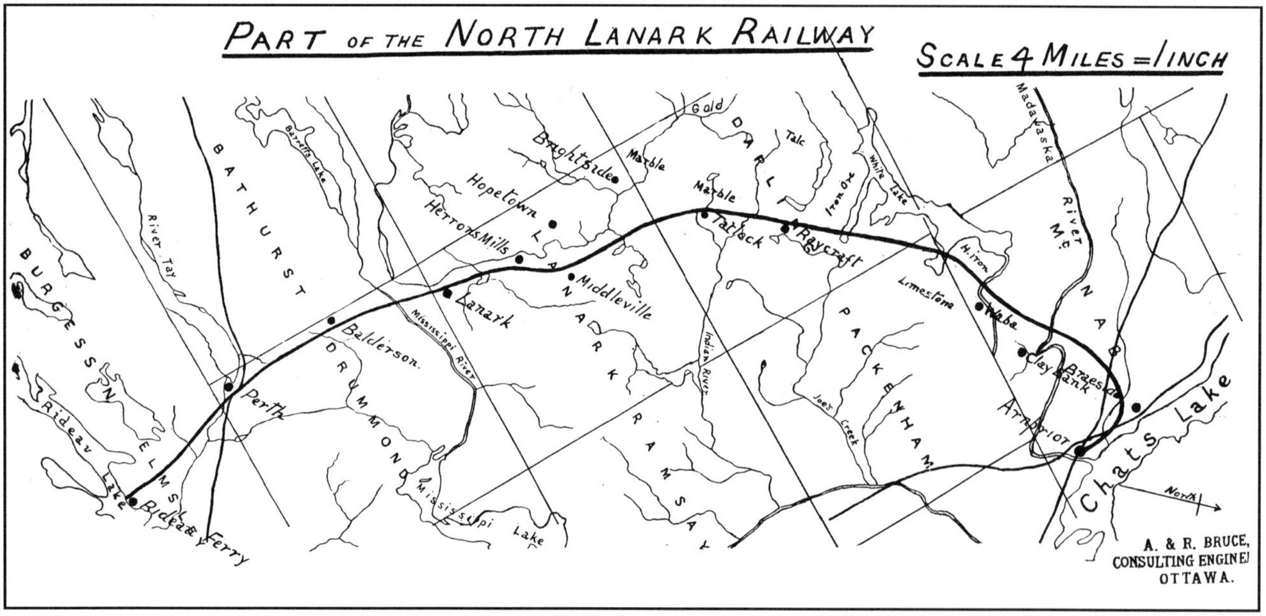

Map of the proposed railway which never came to be. COURTESY OF THE MIDDLEVILLE AND DISTRICT MUSEUM

he was caught. Justice of the day decreed that he be hanged.

Other sinister travellers of the roads robbed families of peace of mind. Grave robbing was not unheard of in days past. More than one grieving father or husband was forced to remain at the grave site for several days, keeping watch over a loved one with a gun. Sometimes a cement slab was placed over the grave to keep the body safe from body snatchers. Medical schools paid well for cadavers and such a ready market kept grave robbers in business.

Two men once dug up a body from a grave and sat the stolen corpse between them on the seat of their buggy. They set off for Kingston. Reining in at a stopping place to get a meal and water their horse, they left the corpse sitting in the buggy. This was a dead giveaway that something was amiss. The two men were apprehended and the body was returned to its place of rest. Other body snatchers in Calabogie were busy at their heinous deed but were forced to decamp hastily when confronted by a group of angry townsmen.

Before cemeteries were set up, burials were done in small family plots at a place in the bush where four lot lines met between farms. The burying ground was shared by the several neighbouring families. Burials were also made at "the foot of the garden" or in the lee of a hill. These lonely sites were especially susceptible to grave robbers.

By 1877, statutes were passed that prevented the interment of the dead within municipalities except at cemeteries. The violation or the defacing of any cemetery stones, buildings or trees was outlawed. There were to be no games or sport played in a cemetery and it was unlawful to disturb persons assembled for the purpose of burying a body.[4]

There were other wily entrepreneurs who covertly went about their business under the cover of darkness. They met their equally stealthy, but sometimes rowdy, customers on the back roads. Bootleggers, with murky bottles of illegal liquor, met thirsty buyers under old pine trees or in obscure pasture laneways to transact their business. One young fellow poled his way across the waters of the Mississippi River in a flat, sap boiling pan to sell his moonshine where he would not be caught near home.

County constables were up against slick customers when they tried to catch bootleggers red-handed. Constable McGregor was one officer always on the look-out for evidence of the operation of a still or a "blind pig" which was an outlet for moonshine.

When a still was discovered, constables moved in to confiscate the tubes and tubs. At one wooded location, they confiscated a load of equipment and carried it through the woods to their waiting buggy out at the road. When they tramped back through the woods to the still for another load, all the remaining equipment had disappeared. They returned to their buggy and found that the confiscated equipment too had been reclaimed by its skulking owner and had disappeared into the bush without a trace.

Despite some illegal selling of liquor, the majority of the log houses in the countryside held law abiding, trusting and trustworthy folk. Their latch strings were always looped outside the door. Strangers and neighbours alike could, at a pull of the string, lift the latch and enter to find warmth or aid. Some rogues and scoundrels took advantage of unsuspecting or innocent folks, but the open door policy of neighbourliness endured over the decades in the countryside.

---

1 Robert Lamond, *A Narrative of the Rise and Progress of Emigration from the Counties of Lanark and Renfrew to the New Settlements of Upper Canada*; (Glasgow, 1821), Canadian Heritage Publications, 1978; p.95.

2 Jean Rankin, Scrapbook, Courtesy of the Middleville and District Museum. Anonymous Poem, *Sixty Years Ago*.

3 The *Perth Courier*, January 29, 1915.

4 *The Revised Statutes of Ontario*, 1877, Chapter 170.

CHAPTER 4

"Needlies and Pinnies" Was the Pedlar's Cry

SUMMER dusts and winter snows saw another type of traveller on the roads – petty chapmen. Buying as well as selling, these itinerant businessmen included pedlars, tinkers and junkmen. They travelled the main roadways as well as the back tracks of distant townships.

As early as 1855, pedlars sold their wares with no duty or licence fee imposed on them. However by 1877, county councils issued licences to travelling salesmen and others carrying on petty trades, who were not permanent residents of Lanark County. A pedlar on foot paid $10. One who drove a single horse paid $20 and there was a charge of $35 for a team. Revenue from the pedlars working in Lanark County at this time was $295. By the turn of the century, pedlars were less numerous and the records of 1908 show that only $105 was collected from "persons following the business of peddling."

Information Wanted

If Wm. Terry who emigrated from Ireland to Montreal about six years ago and there vended goods as a pedlar and is supposed since to have gone to the United States following the same business, be still alive and should chance to see this notice, he would confer a favour on his sister Eliza by addressing a letter to her at Brockville, Upper Canada. Scrapbook newspaper clipping, 1829.

Merchants of many towns were agitating for the formation of businessmen's groups in 1887. They wanted to influence county officials to refuse licences to pedlars of tea, silverware and shoddy or dry goods. Their business interests were being seriously interfered with by the itinerant businessmen but farming families continued to welcome pedlars and hawkers at their doorsteps for many more decades.

To the Warden, &c.:

The undersigned begs leave to report for the information of your Council that since his report to your Council on the 30th day of January, A.D. 1885, the following named parties have received licenses from him up to the present time, viz.:

PEDLARS LICENSES.

A. Goldstein, on foot	$10 00
Wm. Farrell, with one horse	20 00
John Moss, "	20 00
Robt. R. Smith, "	20 00
A. Kennedy, "	20 00
James Thorne, on foot	10 00
Lafarus Watelsky, on foot	10 00
P. Gorman, with two horses	35 00
W. J. Mitchell, with one horse	20 00
Samuel Bermen, "	20 00
M. H. Sh wood, "	20 00
Net total	$205 00

PEDLARS' LICENSES.

John Gafferey, with one horse	$20 00
W. J. Williams, on foot	10 00
Max. Vineberg, with one horse	20 00
Abigail Code, with one horse	20 00
L. Freedman, on foot	10 00
John Bell, on foot	10 00
Total	$90 00

List of pedlars' licences in the *Almonte Gazette*, granted by Lanark County Council as of January 30 and an auxilliary list as of June 1885 including one issued to a business woman.

Dogs always barked at pedlars and excited voices rang out when farm children caught sight of the humpbacked form of the pedlar turning into their laneway. The men were stooped under the weight of the bulky packs they shouldered. Tramping from one place to another through the countryside, the pedlars were welcomed for the bits and bobs of dry goods they carried, as well as for the diversion they brought.

Visitors were rare at the isolated farmsteads in the mid to late 1800s and the early days of the new century. Stores were far away and transportation was slow so the appearance of these travelling men, who carried two eighty-pound packs of merchandise were greeted warmly as they came up the laneway calling out, "Hello. Hello. Needlies and pinnies!"

Surrounded by excited children, the pedlar would wipe his shoes on the mat and step into the farmhouse kitchen. A sack was upended and the contents spilled onto the floor – packets of buttons, hairpins, beads, darning supplies, bright silken embroidery threads, pins and needles. Out came trinkets, decorated hair combs and shiny jewelry pieces: brooches, necklaces and watches. With these small objects came webs of fabric, lengths of oilcloth, tablecloths, ribbons, collars of lace, red handkerchiefs, butter colouring and balls of wick for making candles. The gaudy, printed calicoes rolled in the pack sold for $1.00 per yard – the usual price of an acre of ground! A yard of coarse muslin cost much less.

Some pedlars also carried household remedies in corked bottles with labels promising help for thinning hair, listless children, chapped hands, shattered nerves, sallow complexion, female weakness, and a lack of vital force in men.

Many of these men who peddled through the country were immigrants of Middle Eastern origin. They tramped the roads with their heavy packs and when their fortunes improved they purchased a horse and wagon for their travels. Some even had wagons with a box built on the back with a door which opened at the rear. This could be locked to protect their wares from thieving fingers.

When the merchandise was carried in a wagon, the peddler did not take everything out at each farm. People went to the wagon to view the wares or to ask for specific items. Farm men stopped their field work and ambled over to see what was on offer. Elderly aunts and grandmothers, along with young wives and daughters, swept out in their long skirts to touch the ribbons, inspect the shiny pots and test the strength of bristled brooms. Children skipped about and glimpsed tiny trinkets,

A sketch from the *American Agriculturalist* March 1881 that illustrates the visit of a pedlar to a village home.

wishing covetously for just such a toy soldier or bright ball. After purchases were made or bargains struck and the pedlar's horse was watered, the traveller went on his way.

These travelling salesmen sometimes bartered for items of value that the farmers had to trade. Barter sealed a pedlar's deal in Renfrew County that involved items of significant historical interest. In 1613, the French explorer, Samuel de Champlain lost his astrolabe, a navigating instrument, while making a portage. Two hundred and fifty-four years later the astrolabe was turned up by the blade of a plough when a settler was working a stump-filled field.

Found in close proximity to the astrolabe were two silver cups with a design or engraved crest on them and several small copper pans. The two silver cups were of little use to the farmer or his family and a passing pedlar made a deal and took them off the family's hands. It was later discovered that the two cups were melted down and with them went a bit of Canadian history. The copper pans were later pounded flat and used to patch a crack in a dug-out canoe.[1]

The hardships of tramping ever onward, despite the heat and dust or the rain and cold in mud-clogged tracks, ever on the watch for aggressive farm dogs, must have worn down the pedlar's spirits. They were grateful to slip the packs from their shoulders at day's end, wash up and share a meal with a gracious family. Frequently families shared meals with pedlars even though they had scarcely enough for themselves.

A pedlar's life on the roads was made easier by kindly folks. With two heavy, bulging packs, one pedlar tramped an isolated road to a small settlement called California, in Darling Township. The year was 1916. He approached the King farmhouse and asked if he could have a cucumber from the garden. When given permission by Kate King, he proceeded to eat fourteen cucumbers, with the skins on and all! Obviously he appreciated her friendly generosity.

Lanark's roadways were once tramped by a pedlar with a fine ear for music. One day he stopped at the home of Hugh and Marybelle Munro in Drummond. Noticing a fiddle hanging on the wall he took it down and played a mockingbird tune so well that the family thought the birds were right there in the room. Mr. Munro told him that he could stay overnight at their place any time he was passing by.

Hospitality was always on offer to a Syrian pedlar at the Giles' homestead. After sharing a meal with the family he taught the children the Syrian words for numbers and farm animals. One day, he was talking to Mrs. Giles and she mentioned that there had been another pedlar in the area. He told her some words to say to the fellow the next time he came along. However she was very doubtful as to the meaning or degree of politeness of the suggested phrases.

Pedlars needed to get their horses in some place as night came on. Routes were planned so that hospitable farmsteads were close by at the end of the day. Sometimes they were robbed while they left their wagons to put their horses in a barn for the night, or if their packs were heaped in a corner of a farm kitchen. Unattended goods were easy prey for quick fingers that plucked them out of the sacks and then quickly shoved them under a shirt or into a pocket in a very early form of shoplifting.

After spending a night with a friendly family, the pedlar would leave a small brooch or sweater for the lady of the house and be on his way. Children were sometimes left smiling too, as they sucked on a sweet humbug candy shared out by the traveller as he shouldered his packs or clucked to his horse, snapped the reins and was on the open road again.

In 1912, a pedlar travelled the roads past Tatlock and Hall's Mills. He carried two packs which were so terribly heavy that a strong farmer could hardly lift even one. He stayed over one cold, winter night at the Cameron farmhouse near Hall's Mills and went on his way in the morning. A little later, young William Cameron had to go to Barr's store down the road to get tea for his mother. He hitched his dog to a small hand-sleigh and the well trained dog pulled him along following the right hand track of the snowy winter road. They soon caught up with the pedlar who was also walking in the right hand track. He did not hear them coming along behind him at all. The dog ran right between his legs. The poor man got such a fright that he fell over with both packs into the snow. It was common knowledge that pedlars were always frightened of dogs as they travelled the country roads and this chap thought the dog was certainly going to bite him.

Few of the customers became acquainted with these itinerant salesmen in more than a cursory manner from the short, infrequent visits at farmgates or in village streets. One exception was the Stewart family who ran the mill in Hopetown. They frequently had pedlars stay overnight as they had many extra bedrooms upstairs and gladly shared their home.

Siac Dieb (also spelled Deep) was a favourite of the family and he had a special bond with Myrtle, the young daughter of the household. He told her that he had a sister of the same age back in Syria. He always helped carry wood in for the big woodbox. This was

Syrian pedlars who travelled the roads selling their wares. Seated from left to right are Abdullah, Kahlil and Siac Dieb. Standing, is another relative, Kahlil.
WILSON-CROFT COLLECTION #11103

much appreciated by Myrtle as it was her onerous job to keep the box filled with stove wood.

With a very large soft leather pack full of clothing and fabrics, Siac walked to his customers' far flung farms up in Darling Township. His second pack was a big, wooden box with a carrying strap on it. From this one, he sold combs and trinkets and other hard-edged, breakable objects. He replenished his pack with goods from a relative's store in Carleton Place.

Abdullah, who owned the store in Carleton Place, also furnished merchandise to two other relatives, both of whom were called Kahil. They were differentiated by the names Big Kahlil and Little Kahil. One was Siac's brother and he drove a horse and van through the back lanes and tracks of Dalhousie Township.

In 1908, Siac decided not to stay in Canada and made plans to return to Syria. On his last day in Hopetown, Mrytle was away at school and when she came home she cried because she would never see him again. Her mother let her run to the last house in the village to see if by chance he was still there. Her small feet dashed nimbly down the street but he was gone.

Many lumber companies did not allow "Assyrian pedlars" to enter their camps. However in some shanties, familiar pedlars were welcomed each year and provided a break in a winter evening's routine. It was a profitable encounter for the travelling salesmen as well. Quick selling trinkets were little heart-shaped brooches of mother-of-pearl, with "Sweetheart" or the girl's actual name twisted across it in a pliable gold wire.

In the spring of the year, pedlars made their way to the lumber shanties which were closing up for the season. The lumbermen and teamsters had dollars to spend before they went home and the travelling salesmen knew exactly when to arrive. A big pocket watch, bought in the late 1880s from a pedlar in a shanty, is still kept safely by the McKay family of Rosetta.

Pedlars travelled up the Ottawa Valley to Renfrew on the train with their heavy packs loaded with supplies. Then, selling all along the way, they walked back to Carleton Place or Perth, where they could stock up again. In spite of pedlars being prodigious walkers, there were some farms that never saw their shadows. They were just too far off the beaten track to make it worthwhile for the travellers to walk the miles in.

In the early days of settlement, when farm work was rough and exceedingly demanding, the alternative trade of shoemaking was lucrative and attractive. Shoemakers were itinerant craftsmen who travelled the roads, to even the most isolated farms, in all seasons of the year. The custom of going to individual homes to make shoes was called "whippin' the cat." Each family member had wooden models of their feet, called "lasts," tucked in a chest or on a cupboard shelf, waiting for the annual appearance of the shoemaker. The farmer had to have a supply of tanned leather ready for the visit. The shoemaker pegged the shoes together with wooden pegs because thread rotted in the swampy, muddy conditions of the fields and roads.

In 1870, James Rankin rode his horse to a tannery to get a side of leather and to make arrangements with a shoemaker in Leckie's Corners, near Almonte, to come to his house to make boots for his whole family. He made all the necessary arrangements and with a tanned hide rolled under his arm, he mounted his horse and made his way homeward. He never did see his family in new footwear because he was thrown from his horse as he neared his home in Middleville. He died shortly after from his injuries.

Tin workers, called tinkers, travelled on foot or on horseback. They carried leather sacks with a sampling of their tinware and the tools of the trade. A bedroll and the necessities for a life on the open road were mounded in a back-pack or bumped against the horse's side as they tramped along. Usually considered excellent craftsmen, the tinkers sold tinware and mended pots and pans at farmhouses as they travelled the roads.

Bill Bell tramped from farm to farm, offering his tinkering services for sharpening knives and scissors and repairing pots and sap buckets. Sometimes calling himself Dr. Bell, he found lodging with different families during the coldest part of the winters of the early 1930s. Although considered a general handyman, the Creighton family of Rosetta remember him as being "quite a piece from a doctor." He had a special soldering acid that he made out of hardwood ashes. At David S. Rodger's farm in Rosetta, he uncorked a glass bottle and used a long goose feather dipped in the homemade solution to clean the surface of the sap bucket or pot. It supposedly helped the solder adhere to the metal. Dr. Bell's aspirations of starting a soldering business in the area never panned out as his solder could not always be counted on to stick to the sap pails.

The roads of Lanark County lay before the feet of other traders. A rag man visited farmsteads buying old clothing and rags for a half a cent per pound. He weighed out the used materials on a spring scale, called a set of ouncels, which he drew from his pack. Farm families were always glad to make a bit of money from their cast off, unusable clothing if it was not ripped into strips for rug making. Smallpox was a severe health problem in 1885 and concern was reflected in the *Almonte Gazette*. "What about prohibiting the importation of old rags to the shoddy mill in Almonte from infected districts." An editorial comment reported, "We understand it has been done."

In many stables, two bags or cans were set on a window ledge to hold horsehair groomed from the draught animals. Long tail hair went into one container and the shorter, mane hair into the other. Upholstery businesses needed horsehair to stuff furniture. It was also added to plaster and used for violin bow strings. Alex Erskine, of Rosetta, was a buyer of horsehair, hides and wool. Children earned twenty-five-cent "shin plasters" when they took him bags of hair. These proceeds were often spent on family Christmas presents.

Iron pedlars, or junkmen, travelled from place to place buying up "old done iron." Broken plough points, broken machinery parts and worn out machinery such as seeders, cultivators and straw cutters were piled into wagons and hauled away to a foundry. Rags and old metal had value for a tinsmith in Lanark Village. In 1900, J.H. Wilson advertised, "Cheese factory cans, much improved this season with a heavy, rolled bottom . . . as well as cheese vat relining or repairs. Old metal and rags taken in exchange for tinware."[2]

Farmers peddled stove wood in nearby towns. Buyers had to be wary of any wood pedlars who would not allow an inspection of the wood on the sleigh. Sometimes poor quality wood was piled on the inside of the load.

In the early 1900s, buyers visited farms that had sugar bushes to purchase washed sugar sand. This fine, white sediment, a bi-product of maple sugar making, contained a high level of malate of lime which was used to make baking powder. It sold for prices very close to those of maple sugar at the time but, as it was quite a job to get the sticky sweetness rinsed from the sediment, few farm families found it worth the effort to get it ready for sale.

Occasionally, Indian people travelled along country roadways with a load of handmade baskets of birch bark, grapevines or woven strips of rim ash, heaped in a wagon. Fresh fish was also occasionally on offer. One Indian saleswoman drove a big, chestnut horse from farm to farm long ago. At the Barr farm in Leckie's Corners, she tied her horse to a ring on the side of the woodshed and carried her wares into the big farm kitchen to display her finely worked fancy doilies and edged pillow cases and table-cloths. No one ever knew where this woman came from or who she was. She did her best trade on the outskirts of towns where people had more cash in hand from doing millwork in the factories.

Village blacksmiths and "crossroads smithies" dotted the countryside. They were visited by horseshoe nail salesmen who sold iron bars for forging into implements as well as grooved shoe iron for horseshoes. Coal was available for the forges and an advertisement in the *Carleton Place Herald* of 1859 said – "James Shaw Junior of Smiths Falls offers for sale cheap, fifty chaldrons of the Best Newcastle Double Screened Coals." Wagons heavy with the ingredients for heating iron

W.A. Craig's log Blacksmith Shop, Middleville, 1921. The sign for Massey-Harris Farm Implements above the door on the left foreshadows the coming mechanization of agriculture. It replaced a previous sign over the main door, seen in a 1912 photograph, advertising "Worn Axles Cut Here While You Wait."
COURTESY OF THE MIDDLEVILLE AND DISTRICT MUSEUM

rumbled to blacksmith shops in town and country.

The smithy's forge was a busy place as farmers stopped in to have their horses shod or to get tools or machines fixed. Blacksmiths often worked under pressure because during the planting and harvesting seasons, time was of the essence and every farmer was in a rush to get a broken plough or reaper repaired. In July, 1831, George Easton needed the immediate services of a blacksmith as this diary entry illustrates, "Yesterday broke my scythe to pieces just as my hay was nearly finished."

Anvil Day was celebrated by local blacksmiths. They announced that their places of business would be closed for a day and district members of the guild took time out of their busy rounds to hold meetings to standardize their prices and socialize with their fellow craftsmen. They shared news of improved machinery and in 1900, Mr. A.E. Cunningham, one of the blacksmiths in Middleville, announced that he had added an effective, new implement to his workshop that cut worn buggy axles.

Bruce Edward's blacksmith shop in Drummond Centre, 1909. Three sizes of horseshoes spill luck down over the forge from above the shop door. PA-79049

Notice

We the undersigned Blacksmiths of the district have arranged a new schedule for horseshoeing to take effect on and after the 15th day of Nov. 1912

New Shoes No. 0, 1, 2 at 25c per shoe
New Shoes No. 3 & 4s at 30c per shoe
New Shoes No. 5 & up at 35c per shoe
Resetting Shoes No. 0, 1, 2 at 15c per shoe
Resetting Shoes No. 3 & up 20c per shoe
and 75c per set of 4
Bar shoe 50c per shoe
Resetting bar shoe 25c each

Wm. Haw, Perth
P. Furlong, Perth
J.H. McMillan, Perth
M.P. White, Perth
J. Allan, Scotch Line
Wm. De Witt, Elliot
James Conlon, Glen Tay
Wm. Noonan, Balderson
A. Sheppard, Ferguson's Falls
B. Edwards, Drummond Centre
A. Leighton, Harper
L. Cameron, Fallbrook

A. Buchanan, Playfair
M. McIntyre, Elphin
J. Wilson, McDonald's Corners
S. McIlraith, Lanark
N. Affleck, Lanark
J. Gallinger, Lanark
A. Craig, Middleville
R. Somerville, Middleville
T. Molyneaux, Hopetown
J. Labelle, Watson's Corners
W.J. Wrathall, Poland
E.J. McFarlane, Lavant

(Courtesy of the Lanark & District Museum)

The blacksmith shop was always a place for socializing and this bit of an old poem describes the atmosphere.

The village blacksmith, so they say
Is never lonesome through the day.
He greets each caller with a grin
And welcomes all the loafers in.[3]

Journeymen travelled the roadways taking their skills and equipment wherever they were in demand. In the mid 1800s, there were loom fixers and barn builders, bricklayers and stone masons on the roads. Stone cutters also travelled to job sites to engrave cemetery headstones and cut chimney thimbles or collars that encircled stove pipes where they passed through floor boards. Wooden pump salesmen,

The first blacksmith shop in Hopetown. It was a busy place from the 1830s until it was replaced in 1917. Advertisements for Bickmore's Gall Cure and McLean, the tailor from Lanark Village are tacked on the front of the shop.
PA-9097 WILSON-CROFT COLLECTION

Perth Marble Shop.

THE subscriber begs to intimate to the inhabitants of Perth and surrounding townships that he is now manufacturing from New York and Vermont Marble, plain and ornamental

HEAD STONES & TOMB STONES

Also, all kinds of MONUMENTS and CHIMNEY PIECES will be executed to order; and all orders from the county punctually attended to.
Moderate charges made for all kinds of work.

JOSIAH DAVIES

Perth, Jan 20, 1857. 15m

Deaths in families brought other travellers onto the roads. Professionally made headstones or marble tombstones were ordered and delivered to well-to-do families. Other graves were marked with field stones, wooden crosses or maple or oak saplings. *PERTH COURIER*, 1857

ploughmen and wood choppers answered advertisements in the newspapers and followed the call to work from place to place.

Some young women left home at an early age to do domestic work in towns. Many travelled between homes in their districts to spin, weave or do dressmaking. Young women also helped support their families by doing field work during harvest time.

Prospectors tramped the roads of the back country, poking and prodding into the earth and rock to find their fortunes. Some of the valuable claims that were staked held deposits of copper, iron, feldspar, calcite, graphite and phosphate as well as silver, gold and mica. The prospecting provided employment opportunities for young women as well as men. The *Lanark Era* of 1904 carried this advertisement, "Girls to clean mica; good wages, steady work. Apply to General Electric Company, Cleaning House, Box 70, Perth."

Pioneers of photography were other businessmen on the roads. Photographers were welcomed at farmhouses because families wanted their houses, gardens and horses as well as their faces recorded for all time. The phrase "watch the birdie" was heard as families, "all togged up" in their Sunday clothes, sat for the picture-taking sessions. A small brass bird with a movable beak and wings was attached beside the camera. The photographer animated it by squeezing a rubber bulb just before the picture was snapped to get more animated facial expressions. Many were the family photographs that crossed the Atlantic Ocean for relatives back in the home country.

A diary entry by Joseph Tennant on January 18, 1887 illustrates the impact of the photographer's presence on his hard working farm family. ". . . Mr. Duff, a photographer, being here we did not do much."

R.J. Stead was a photographer in Lanark Village from the 1870s, on to the turn of the century. He did a good trade in tintypes which had recently been invented and being of a scientific bent he understood the chemical processes involved. He drove a horse and two-wheeled cart to serve customers around the district. However, his best trade was in the spring when the lumber camps broke up and the shanty men hastened smilingly to the studio to have their pictures taken.

Tramps were not an unusual sight on the country roads through the years. However, they were seen more frequently when a large number of young men took to tramping or

☛ SOMETHING NEW IN PHOTOGRAPHY. Mr. R. J. Stead is prepared to take flash-light photographs of offices, parlors, groups, lodges and all kind of interior work. By notifying me parties living in the country will receive prompt attention.

Robert Stead travelled the roads in a two-wheeled cart to photograph his customers. *LANARK ERA,* APRIL, 1898

DAGUERREOTYPE

MINIATURES.

W. CROFT

Would respectfully inform the Ladies and Gentlemen of and vicinity, that he has taken Rooms

where he is prepared to take

DAGUERREOTYPE LIKENESSES,

in the latest and most improved style, with or without colors, and warranted not to fade or change by age.

☞ Ladies and Gentlemen are particularly invited to call at his rooms and examine his Specimens, whether they intend to have likenesses or not.

MINIATURES PUT UP

in Cases, Lockets Rings or Bosom Pins, or any size desired.

Hours for operating, from 8 A. M., till 5 P. M.

☞ Mr. C. will tarry but a few days in this place.

New technology came to towns and villages in the form of daguerrotypes. W. Croft advertised the opportunity to have a likeness done in the latest style with or without colour. Miniatures could be ordered in lockets, small cases, rings or bosom pins. Poster circa 1900.
COURTESY OF THE MIDDLEVILLE AND DISTRICT MUSEUM

wandering the roads after the First World War. Demobilization set men free without trades and the field of casual employment could not absorb them all. Many men, having suffered through the trauma of war, could not settle long enough in one place to find work or contentment. Tramps were wayfarers on the roads of Lanark County who were not welcomed at every farmgate.

These wanderers were the greatest fear of any woman left alone and children too felt very wary of them. Some kind-hearted women wanted to feed the men to help them out, but they never wanted to be alone in the house with one of them. Children were told to keep their eyes open and if they saw anyone entering their house they were to come straight in themselves. It was an important job for a child if the mother was a generous woman but nervous of the travellers. Other women "put the run on" the tramps and were rarely visited. Some mark at the road alerted the men that there was no hospitality to be had up that lane.

There were some farmsteads where kindliness and hospitality were sacred bonds. Friends, neighbours, agents and pedlars – all were invited in for "a wee bite to eat." Tramps who chanced upon these generous souls were lucky and welcomed the warm food and tea before they went on their tramping way.

Tramps stayed overnight with families who would have them, but often they had to find a sheltered spot out of doors. Close-growing cedar groves, with deep, soft layers of needles on the ground were sheltering places where travelling men spent the night by the wayside. One summer night a weary tramp slept on a

Two studio photographs of men with the tools of their trades. Circa 1890. Photographer unknown. COURTESY OF THE MIDDLEVILLE AND DISTRICT MUSEUM

flat rock at Lane's Corners, on the Galbraith Road. In the morning, he came to the nearby Munro house asking for a lunch to carry. Mrs. Munro kindly made him up a sack and he went off to pick up the thread of his journey.

> "The whole Ottawa Valley is overrun by tramps and they are having things all their own way!"
>
> *Renfrew Mercury*, July, 1889.

Farm families usually had a rule that any tramps who slept in their back kitchens or in their attics had to turn over their matches and tobacco for the night. Perhaps stories of careless smoking, like the one in the *Almonte Gazette* of 1900, fostered a mistrust of tramps. "One farmer was absent from his farm, being away at a [religious] camp meeting. While he was away, his barn was destroyed by fire, supposed to be caused by tramps."

Some families did not encourage tramps to stop at their farms at all. Mrs. Jack Brown was said to have "a heart as big as a cow" – if she liked you. One summer day, she was standing by her screen door sharpening a long butcher knife for slicing the meat at dinner. A tramp came along and she sternly asked, "Did anyone see you come in the gate? — Well, if you don't go quick, no one will see you go out!"

A tramp named Peter McLaughlin got in the habit of coming to Robert and Agnes Pretty's farmhouse too often, just at meal time. One day, the family saw him coming and everyone hid in a bedroom and did not answer the rap at the door. After peeking out a window and seeing the tramp departing down the lane, they came out and began their meal. Suddenly, he was back at the door and said, "Dang it. You can't fool Peter. Get me a plate. I saw the smoke coming out of your chimney."

Stopping at a nice village home one day, a travel-worn tramp asked the lady of the house if she could spare some change. She said that she had none to spare and he replied sarcastically, "Then you had better sell your house, because you are obviously living far beyond your means!"

Tramps frequently visited hotels or stopping places where alcohol was sold and they begged for drinks. One old fellow appealed politely, "Would you kindly give a poor, downhearted man something to drive dull care away?" The bartender answered with a twinkle in his eye, "I'm disposed to be generous," and pushing a small dish toward him, said, "Here, help yourself to a caraway seed!"

Studies of two affectionate women in their voluminous black skirts of the day and a jaunty young woman of a later generation. Photographer unknown.

COURTESY OF THE MIDDLEVILLE AND DISTRICT MUSEUM

An old man called Grundy was a well known tramp in Lanark and Ramsay Townships. Walking with a slump and carrying a stick with a wee bag on the end of it, he travelled the roads before and after the First World War. He visited farms for handouts both summer and winter. Many people thought he was a spy but he claimed to be interested in mining. He dug holes in the back country and is reputed to have found an iron deposit.

Every so often, a neighbour would inform a member of the Creighton family of Rosetta, that they would soon be having a visitor. Then they knew to expect Grundy, who had been seen sitting on a stump down the road waiting for dinnertime to come. It was the custom at William and Ellen Creighton's house to take in travelling folk and their hospitality was always on offer. "Grundy's quilt," which was made from heavy woolen pieces from the shoddy mill, was always kept folded on a shelf for his overnight stays.

Grundy was a civil man and when asked if he wanted more at a meal, he always replied with a swift, "No thanks, yes, maybe I will." For breakfast he usually requested "just a bit of an egg," although the family wondered what he thought they would do with the rest of the egg.

Children found him very gruff. One evening, at the Giles' farm, he was very put out because there were biscuits instead of bread for supper and he let the young women of the family know it. He is also supposed to have told a youngster who was sweeping up after dinner that, "It wasn't polite to sweep when someone was eating." He was the only one not finished his tea yet. Everyone else had gone back to work.

Grundy travelled a regular route around the countryside, stopping each night at the places where he knew he was welcome. He never worked for any of the meals that he was given, although perhaps he shared a song with the families. A story was told that, "he had been a trained singer at one point in his life but had got away from that and started tramping the roads." He tramped the Lanark County roads until the end of his life. News came back to the communities where his face was familiar that he had died in Perth but the details of his last days were never learned.

Long before Grundy's days on the roads, vagrants were an expense to the county. In 1885, County Council reported the cost as: Committal of Vagrant, $25.00, Coffin for Vagrant, $33.25 and Digging grave, $1.50. Perhaps Grundy was one of the vagrants who received assistance and then a burial from the county officials in later years when he was aged and infirm.

---

[1] Henry Scadding, "The Astrolabes of Samuel Champlain and Geoffrey Chaucer," *Rose Belford's Canadian Monthly and National Review*, Volume 5, Number 6, (December, 1880), p.589.
[2] The *Lanark Era*, April 11, 1900.
[3] Mrs. J.R. Reid, Scrapbook, Courtesy of the Middleville and District Museum; Anonymous Poem.

CHAPTER 5

From Farm to Farm

NEIGHBOURHOOD traffic patterns were predictable and routine. Local commerce flowed along the roads like an ever running stream and people could set their clocks by the mail carrier. Keeping track of one's neighbours by casting a watchful eye on the roads was an avocation for some but a compulsive pastime for others who were intent on knowing all that went on in the community.

Turnip seeders, potato planters and hillers, ploughs, harrows, two-wheeled dump wagons and other farm implements were frequently moved between neighbouring farms. They were shuttled back and forth, shared by several families. Harvest loads were part of the road traffic too as crops were cut and transported home. Lumbering loads of sweet smelling hay from the fields of summer were taken home to stack in convenient places near barnyards. It was not always easy to maneuver bulky hay wagons down the narrow, rutted concession roads. In 1858, the attention of a township council was directed to a concession line where the brush had encroached up on the road until it was almost impossible to drive a load of hay through.

From May until November, early morning trips were made to the many cheese factories that were located every four miles or so. With full milk cans strapped in the back of farm wagons, the farmers delivered milk to the factories. They wanted to make the trip in good time so they could get back home to put in a full day of farm work. Some farmers picked up many neighbours' milk cans. No one wanted to have to wait while all the milk cans from a milk route were being weighed in ahead of them. This led to some hasty drives, with milk cans rattling, if a person with a large load was spotted coming along the road. Sometimes such races resulted in upsets with milk cans rolling and milk splashing in the dust.

Patrons of the cheese factories took turns drawing cheese in the summertime. Every two

The patrons lined up to deliver their milk to the Middleville Cheese Factory, 1902. Built in 1888, it burned in 1929 but was rebuilt at a different site and back in operation within two months. PA- 91028

weeks or so, a wagon-load of up to thirty-six cheeses had to be delivered to the nearest railway station. Each of the cheeses weighed approximately ninety pounds so the loads made heavy work for the horses. An added small burden was the weight of several children perched on top of the cheese boxes as their father drove to the station. Going into town was always a special treat for children who rarely travelled farther than the farmgate, except to go to church or the school down the road.

Cheese box factories were set up around the countryside and did a steady trade, as every cheese factory needed hundreds and hundreds of boxes each season. Large, heavy loads of elm logs were delivered to the busy box-making factories to be soaked in boiling water and then split for the manufacture of the round boxes and their lids. Bulky loads of cheese boxes were delivered in wing rack wagons to the many cheese factories that dotted the townships.

With the opening of the first cheese factories in the 1870s, farm families received cash for their milk. It was the first money that they could regularly count on. No longer did they have to rely on trading wool, homemade cheese, maple sugar or other farm produce for groceries and dry goods.

A busy morning at the Hopetown Cheese Factory. The farmers weighed in their milk under the protective roof on the left. The round whey tank is on the right. Built in 1884, the factory served the community farmers until 1933.
COURTESY OF THE MIDDLEVILLE AND DISTRICT MUSEUM

Well-provisioned stores were important centres of supply and demand for homesteading families throughout the countryside. An 1882 periodical gave this description, "Cow-bells were strung on a row of nails in the beams of the ceiling; a few ox-bows hung on the wall; a barrel full of axe handles, a spinning-wheel and reel were set out as a sample of more in the 'store house;' a box of gun flints on the counter; pieces of moleskin trousering and pieces of satinette and as many of homespun flannel for shirting on the shelves."[1]

Young men and old spent their idle hours leaning on the counters and sitting on nail kegs and vinegar barrels behind the stove, until the wooden tops were worn to a bright finish. Discussions about horse trades, local and church politics as well as opinions about the crops, the weather and any romantic suits underway were all voiced in animated tones. In the evening, when the smoky lanterns were blown out and the door was firmly locked by the storekeeper, the farmers unhitched their horses from nearby fences and headed homeward. As the men walked into their kitchens ". . . the same effect was produced as the delivery of an individual mail-bag at every house."[2]

One piece of news always set tongues wagging and made parents hope against hope that one of their own family was not involved. This was the quickly circulated report that some likely looking youth had been seen "on the road to Perth." It had but one significance. One more stalwart from the clean hills of the upcountry was setting out, possessed by the desire to achieve fame and fortune out west or in a city factory. The young lads, satchels in hand and high hopes in their hearts took the road to Perth and it was blamed for draining the Clyde country of its strong, virile youth.[3]

Youthful visions of adventure and riches to be found out west or in the Klondike beckoned young men in the late 1800s and the early 1900s. Large numbers of seasonal workers were needed in the wheat fields of the prairies so special harvest excursion trains were put on. All across the country, lads headed west to the wide fields of ripe grain. Many returned to kith and kin at the end of the harvest but others did not. They decided to settle in the west and called wives and sweethearts to follow.

An advertisement for field workers in the *Carleton Place Herald* in August, 1919.

While some men set out for far flung places to make a living, others chose to work to improve the lot of farmers at home. They attended meetings to set up branches of an agricultural association called the Grange of Patrons of Husbandry. It was a secret farmers' society set up to help them circumvent large companies and get seed and insurance at a good rate as well as to encourage cooperation in agriculture. The Rosetta Grange, Charter 788 was running in 1889 and dealt with The Grange Wholesale Supply Company of Toronto. The Grange association did not last long but many chartered groups did make a start in Lanark County. The movement made a reappearance in later years as the United Farmers of Ontario.

"Egg circles" were organized in the early 1900s and met at local community or agricultural halls. The farmers of the MacDonalds Corners area formed their local egg marketing cooperative in 1908. Each farm family stamped its farm number on its eggs with a little rubber stamper. The eggs, packed in specially made wooden, slatted, buggy egg crates, were taken to the egg circle one evening a week. Some farmers arrived with as many as twelve dozen eggs, all carefully placed under the back seat of the buggy. The districts' eggs were loaded into wagons and delivered to town merchants. Payment was made to the farmers at the next meeting after the eggs were sold.

Stock was driven along the roads to markets, to the train station or to new owners. Lambs, turkeys, hogs and cattle were driven to towns to be sold. The drovers had to be vigilant to keep the creatures from straying into every yard or garden along the way. As well they had to watch the condition of their charges. Turkeys got foot sore and lame when driven along stony roads. Small leather boots were sometimes fitted on their feet or their feet were dipped in pine pitch and then coated with sand.

The *Almonte Gazette* reported the hazards of moving animals and one solution that was found:

> August 28, 1885
> Two large hogs, belonging to John Houston of Ramsay, died from exhaustion while being driven to Carleton Place Station last Friday morning.
>
> August 31, 1900
> Mr. T. J. Bole, the enterprising butcher in Almonte, has added to his outfit a "pallace car" in which he conveys livestock to his slaughter house. It saves both time and labour and in hot weather, animals are brought in in much better condition than when driven along the roads.

A good cattle dog saved farm families lots of shoe leather on the roads. The men could follow their cattle to market in a buggy and their dogs did all the work keeping the beasts moving. One day a trusted family dog ducked off the road as it was driving cattle. When the owner followed it, he found a dead sheep. Not wanting to believe his valued dog was a sheep killer he whistled it back to its herding job. However, several days later it was found with wool in its mouth and was shot on the spot. Another suggested cure for a dog with such a problem was to "cut its tail off close to its ears."

> 1872 advice in the *Almonte Gazette.* " Bells are considered good for the preservation of sheep flocks from marauding dogs. The value of a single sheep would purchase quite a number of bells and they should be the noisy rattle-de-bang type not little tinkling things full of pastoral, poetic melodies."

Dogs were valued workers on the homesteads. A faithful collie served its master with strong herding and protective instincts. Every day it was left with the two family cows as they grazed on the side of the public road. It allowed nothing to interfere with them and then at milking time the dog could be seen herding them home without the aid of a child as driver.

Sows were driven to boars at nearby farms and cows to neighbours' bulls. The trading of labour or goods for the stud services was the usual transaction but cash did sometimes figure in the equation. In March, 1909, A.W. Baird, a farmer from Lanark Township, imported a bull from Winchester. The tired and confused animal was led down the ramp at the Perth train station and firmly hitched behind the farm wagon. He was led the long miles to his new home. New bloodlines in the community were much sought after and the bull proved to be a good source of revenue for the Baird family.

As ox power gave way to horse power on the roads and in the fields, stallions were needed to improve the bloodlines of the farm draught horses. Large and lovely purebred Percheron, French Canadian and Clydesdale stallions were "travelled" around the country-side. Route bills, nailed to trees at crossroads or tacked to local blacksmiths' doors, advertised the places that a stallion and his handler would be stopping. Every week or so in the spring and early summer, the stallions were led behind a single buggy to selected farms. The stallion handler stayed for lunch at one place, and overnight at the next and the farmers would "call in with their mares." The stud fee of $10 was owed when the mare proved to be in foal.

Farm records and accounts were meticulously kept at some homesteads. James Rankin's 1872 record book delicately noted stock breeding dates like this: Peggy got the horse. Lilly met a young animal at home. Spot got young French Canadian of Playfair's - single service $3.50.

Around 1908, King, a big, darkly dappled grey Percheron stallion was travelled in the

TO OWNERS OF

ENTIRE  HORSES.

ROUTE BILLS

EXECUTED in the best manner, and at short notice, at the

"ALMONTE EXPRESS" OFFICE.

A new and beautiful Horse Cut just received from the Montreal Type Foundry.

May 31, 1861. 2-tf.

Stallions (often referred to as 'entire horses') were travelled from farm to farm to service mares. "Route bills" were ordered to advertise the dates of their route through the countryside. The small one is from the *Almonte Gazette* in 1861 while the larger one indicating more regulations, is from the *Perth Courier* in 1915.

HORSEMEN

Now is the time to order

Route Cards and Folders

Under the new regulations of the Stallion Enrollment Board, horsemen are compelled to have their horses inspected and enrolled.

Sec. 12 (2)—Every poster issued shall contain a copy of the certificate of enrolment printed in bold face and conspicuous type and shall not contain any illustrations, pedigrees or other matter which is untruthful or misleading.

This Office is prepared to execute all orders to comply with the regulations.

THE COURIER

Almonte area. His dapples were like fifty-cent pieces, all over his hide. He was a fine stallion and as a consequence there were lots of dappled grey teams in the Ramsay Township, Middleville and Rosetta areas. However, the stallions were not kept for too many seasons in one area - two or three at the most - and then they were traded or sold to keep new bloodlines in the local stock.

Sample of a stallion advertisement in the *Almonte Gazette* in June, 1885.

People were proud of their animals and always enjoyed beating a neighbour at a fair. From the very earliest days of settlement, agricultural "showfairs" drew streams of people from around the countryside to their crowded grounds for a great social gathering. Animals were driven down the rutted roads to the exhibition grounds. Cattle ambled along, their numbers swelling as others joined in on the way to the fair. Sows woofed at piglets that darted along the road and scooted through any available hole in a fence. Glossy teams of horses trotted out smartly, pulling wagons filled with crates of hens, turkeys and geese. Excited children with new hair ribbons or new hats sat on the wagon seats holding their exhibits carefully on their laps.

Livestock competitions were held throughout the afternoon. The prizes handed out were shyly yet proudly received. Prize money was often used to pay farm property taxes. Money won for cakes, rolls of butter, wool, homespun cloth, maple sugar, cookies and socks was added to livestock winnings to pay the dreaded tax man and thus keep the wolf from the door for another year.

Winning beasts were often sold for good sums of money. A diary entry written after a fair in 1838, told of George Easton's successful outing. "This day Dalhousie Fair, plenty of grog and beer. I sold my oxen to J.B., Price £12 - 15*s*." Showfairs were always sources of great relaxation. Everybody thought himself specially licensed on such occasions, and nearly every man got drunk.

The afternoon of the fair was filled with visiting among friends and neighbours as well as chasing livestock that inevitably got loose from time to time causing much hilarity in the catching. As the shadows lengthened, everyone gathered up families, exhibits and beasts and with calls of farewell on the evening air, started for home. The cattle did not need to be driven

From the early days of settlement agricultural showfairs drew people together for a social day of friendly competition.

COURTESY OF THE MIDDLEVILLE AND DISTRICT MUSUEM

home. They went along by themselves and the older children followed in the dark, perhaps walking with sweethearts or in a group of chums. Fair day was always "a big time out for everyone".

The success of the showfairs was at the whim of nature and man. The North Lanark Fair directors thought they had "a peach of a fair" planned in 1896 with a trick bicycle riding demonstration and a balloon ascension. However, the Wednesday afternoon of the fair was very disappointing. The gate receipts came in severely under expectations due to a Canadian Pacific Railroad workers' strike which deprived hundreds of fair goers of transportation. Torrential rains on Tuesday spoiled the roads and kept many others at home as well.

Heavy weather and bad roads rarely affected church attendance. In all seasons, come rain or shine, Kirk day or Sunday saw the roads busy with families on foot or in horse drawn vehicles on their way to their local churches. The mud holes and boggy, rutted roads of spring stopped few from attending church for spiritual guidance and a chance to visit with friends and relations. Families tramped long miles through the bush and swale to attend church, often carrying their shoes until they neared the village to save shoe leather. Worshippers trooped in and the churches bulged with large families each filling long, straight pews. Religion was an important part of life and no effort to get to church was too great.

In the winter, warmly dressed families trudged along the snowy roads or were bundled under buffalo robes in a sleigh, with hot bricks at their feet. If snow-drifts blocked the roads, panels of rail fences were taken out to allow an easier path through the fields.

In the early days of settlement around Rosetta, in Lanark Township, church services were held at a large rock outcropping called the Preaching Rock. People walked miles to the Sabbath gatherings held there. One cold, spring day, a woman with a small baby trudged along the bush trails to get to a service. In her concern for her wee one she bundled it up warmly. When she got to the Preaching Rock, she found that the baby had smothered during the trip. One can only guess at the deep sorrow and desperate pain the woman suffered, living so far away from kith and kin, deep in the forest of early Lanark.

From the backwoods of the county the pioneers made their way to the Presbyterian church in Lanark Village. In 1841, it had a faithful and devout following of one hundred and seventy members. Some of the men and women travelled many miles on horseback to worship while others came by oxcart from shorter distances. Often large communion services were held which attracted worshippers from up to thirty miles away. These gatherings followed a common custom in the Highlands of Scotland where people worshipped with neighbouring congregations at special sacramental services.

After the sermons were over, the pews emptied and people stood about talking with

Rosetta's Preaching Rock where open-air services were held by the first Scottish settlers in the area is located on Lot 13 Concession 9 of Lanark Township.

CLAUDIA SMITH

The Drummond Baptist Church built in 1891 at a three-way crossroads in the countryside.

COURTESY OF THE MIDDLEVILLE AND DISTRICT MUSEUM

their friends and neighbours. The horses were untied and harnesses were tightened for the homeward trek. Spirited horses grew impatient if they were kept standing while families visited together. They would strike out for home as soon as the family was aboard and they were given their heads. At the Elphin church, it was the thrill of the week to see Issac Allan's sleek, black horse take off from the church yard. Young men of the congregation held the horse's tossing head while Mrs. Allan took a flying leap into the buggy seat beside her husband and they were off in a rattle of stones and a roll of dust.[4]

While driving home from an uplifting church service one Sunday morning, a family encountered one of those beautiful, striped-backed creatures of the countryside. The little skunk would not move out of the way and the farmer had to take his own part of the road where he could get it. The result was that well known stench on the air and extra work for the dressmakers and tailors in town.[5]

Sundays also saw some worshippers walking many miles to a church far away from the home village. Disenchantment with the minister or the policies of their congregations made some of the rigidly moral members fall out with their local churches.

The Catholic church was not immune to disenchantment by its parishioners. Paddy O'Keefe, a poverty stricken homesteader, could not afford to buy a pew seat so every Sunday he carried a block of wood to sit on. The priest often criticized him for not paying. One Sabbath Paddy had had enough of it. He got up, chucked the block of wood in the stove and walked out. The church lost a member of its congregation as the man never darkened its door again.

Sundays were always looked forward to as a time to "go calling." Women prepared food on Saturday to be ready for any friends or relations coming to call. Potatoes were peeled and cakes, pies and bread were baked to accompany the canned pork, beef and chicken that stood in jars in the cellar ready for any numbers that should arrive. Older daughters still at home baked all day Saturday and probably with discouragement noted there was very little left by Monday. The children knew that there could be no fishing, games, whistling or running about on the Sabbath. The visits ended with pots of strong tea and organ or piano music and hymn singing in the parlour.

Many congregations were required to call at the manse on certain days of the year to pay the preacher. The stipends paid to priests and ministers consisted of wheat, oats, hay, maple sugar, wool, vegetables, candles, potatoes and other vegetables. The pioneer families gave what they could to support their church and its leaders, but in the early days very little cash was paid out for the enlightenment of the soul.

Before 1830, Alexander Watt of Dalhousie Township taught school in the village of Poland and at Hart's School near Lammermoor, sharing his time between them during the winter months. History handed down by word of mouth tells of teacher-preachers travelling the forest tracks of Lanark County before 1849. One learned man travelled by horseback to various communities on different nights of the week. He arrived at the small log school houses to teach the children for a couple of hours. Children, eager for book learning, looked forward to his arrival and were always punctual. This travelling teacher taught the sturdy farm children their ABCs and moral development by the flickering light of a bog rush lamp or a tallow candle set in a lantern.

> Schools were often the first public buildings erected in the tiny settlements. In some families, grandfathers took small children on their knees and taught them the alphabet from a dish that had letters around the rim.

Many of the settlers valued education and had a thirst for intellectual stimulation. John Climie was pleased to report back to his family in Scotland about his new house in the new land. He was an educated man and his letter reflects his priorities in his furnishings. "I have got up my house which is 16 feet by 20, and two stooped beds, of my own making, and a case for my library, and a shelf for the dishes."[6]

In the Granny Cummings' Corners area (Watson's Corners) the people were fortunate to have a library in their community from the very earliest days. Lord Dalhousie, Governor-in-Chief of Canada, was petitioned for help and he donated many volumes as well as a set of the Encyclopedia Brittanica to the people of the District of Bathust. The donated books were housed in a library in a log meeting place called

A rough, rural road passing through Watson's Corners. Circa 1890. A family is captured on film near a stand where a cheese factory can full of milk is waiting to be picked up. Children's rocking horses, a rocking chair and a cat on the big veranda set a pleasant scene on this early postcard. COURTESY OF THE MIDDLEVILLE AND DISTRICT MUSEUM

St. Andrew's Hall. As early as 1829, the educating influence of this collection of books spread to the sons and daughters of the first settlers as well as satisfying the literary needs of the older generation.

The rough trails from nearby farms and communities were busy on Library Day as people walked to this library. People from Lavant, thirteen miles away, gladly tramped the roadways to exchange their books. Residents of the older settlement of Hopetown also trekked to Watson's Corners on Library Day. Along the way, people met relatives and neighbours and exchanged news and greetings. George Easton's 1830s diary entries show that "Library Issue" day was not a date to forget even in the busy round of pioneering life.

Young hitch-hikers found intellectual stimulation while riding on crunching sleigh runners with William Mooney, a friendly cordwood teamster from Pakenham. Every Friday the boys would get a ride home from school on his sleigh, which had been emptied of its load at the wood yard. Mr. Mooney always had a copy of the *Almonte Gazette* and sat in the sleigh reading every word of it to the youngsters, trusting the reins to them. The kids were delighted and they heard all about what the editor, the Honourable William Templeton thought and they were told that every word he wrote was just about right.

Friendly teamster John Hudson gave the youngsters of the Pakenham countryside great enjoyment as well. He was not a formally educated man but was a wonderful poet. He sat on his sleigh, with his young hitch-hikers as the team headed homeward, and spun out his poems and yarns, casting a spell over his listeners.

More sombre occasions on the roadways were the long lines of buggies that fell in behind a big, black horsedrawn funeral coach as it wound its way over the hills and twists of a dusty road, to a small family burying ground on a distant farm or to a church cemetery. There were many superstitions connected with funerals and dying. It was a commonly held belief that if there was an extra space left between two vehicles in a funeral procession then another funeral would soon follow. It was also considered the worst kind of bad luck to count the number of rigs in a funeral procession. However, a long line of mourners behind a hearse showed the esteem in which the deceased was held. Attendance at funerals was appreciated by bereaved families but processions of sixty-five rigs or more were uncommon. The hearse carrying the body of Mrs. Matthew Riddell of the Fitzroy area was followed by two hundred and thirty carriages. In some communities a cortege was not measured in rigs but rather in length. One procession was supposed to have been two miles long.

> Almonte undertaker, T.E. Seaman, advertised the rates for the use of his hearse in the *Almonte Gazette* in 1872, "all funerals in the village, attended with a single horse, cost three dollars. A team cost five dollars. Funerals in the country, less than six miles from town, with a double team in service, cost six dollars. All scarfs, gloves etc. were furnished without extra charge." He had ready-made coffins, coffin trimmings and shrouds as well as metallic coffins available when required.

When the inevitable summons from the "pale horse and rider" came to an old resident of the locality, a team of black horses pulled the hearse. A team of sombre greys was harnessed for a young person's funeral. Another symbol in the funeral procession was a detachable, black wooden cross which stood on the roof of the hearse for a Roman Catholic funeral and was taken off for a Protestant one. Many floral tributes were sent in memory of the deceased. The Broken Circle arrangement was made for a spouse who passed away and the floral cross was the tribute for one's child. Other arrangements put in hearses around coffins were called Gates Ajar, Pillow, and Anchor. Sheaves of ripe grain were sometimes placed on coffins or rough boxes to honour the deceased.

An 1885 advertisement for undertaking services in the Almonte area.

Advertisement for furniture and undertaking services in the *Perth Courier* in 1877. D. Hogg had coffins of walnut and rosewood. Shrouds and trimmings were available to suit all needs. At this point the hearse was a wagon.

In an 1887 diary entry, Joseph Tennant of Halpenny noted, "Went to Johnny's wake. Helped coffin him." People were waked and buried from their homes. Contingents of relatives and neighbours came to pay their respects to the family and to the deceased in the coffin in the parlour. Summertime wakes necessitated many buckets of ice under the casket to keep the corpse cool in the hot weather. A wide black and purple crape rose, with long, hanging ribbons, was pinned to the door of a house where a body was laid out. It warned anyone approaching that the family was in mourning.

Some family cemetery plots were in a corner of a field near a special tree or on a knoll. Sometimes a loved one was buried at the foot of the garden, with the neighbours and relatives gathered around for the service. One old man, lying near death, requested that he be buried "in a link of the snake fence where they [would not] be geein' and hawin' the oxen over [him]."

George Young owned the hearse used in the Lanark Township area for many years.

COURTESY OF ALATHEA NAIRN

Funerals in the wintertime were especially hard for the bereaved families if the roads were blocked with snow. Driving teams of plunging horses through snow- drifts was not conducive to calming the nerves of grieving people. Relatives had great difficulty reaching the farms to give comfort or aid. In February, 1887 Joseph Tennant noted, ". . . went to a funeral. Went on snowshoes the road being blocked off."

No wheels rolled in the winter. The funeral coach was put on a set of sleighs or "sloops" to navigate on the winter roads. The undertakers, bundled in big, fur coats, were exposed to all sorts of weather as they rode perched on the high hearse seats. The entourage of sleighs and cutters wound to the cemetery if the cold ground allowed for grave digging, or to a vault if the earth was as hard as iron.

When the roads were sealed so it was impossible for the hearse to get through, the bereaved family sometimes transported the coffin on a set of sleighs. This unsatisfactory arrangement sometimes saw the coffin slip off into the snow drifts. Even when there was no snow on the ground, accidents could happen. One slushy spring day the funeral coach was needed for two funerals and in the rush, a corner in Clayton was taken too fast and the hearse tipped right over, but with no damage done.

Poor weather was not the only circumstance that heaped sorrow upon sorrow for those in mourning. When disease struck a family, their farm was placed under quarantine. John Crawford, of Darling Township, had a five-year-old child taken away by the dreadful hand of diphtheria and no neighbours dared come to help bury the little one. A young man named Majaury undertook the burial and with horse and sleigh, removed the body to the cemetery near Hopetown. However he was unable to lower the coffin into the grave without assistance so he had to return his sombre load from whence it came. The child was later buried with another sibling who had the germs of the same trouble.

> Horse power continued to be used for funerals for many years. In 1938, the undertaking department of W.J. Jackson, of MacDonald's Corners, advertised that caskets would be delivered anywhere on short notice and that both motor and horsedrawn hearses were always in readiness.

Funerals were not the only time people came to each other's aid. If someone was injured in an accident, neighbours were quick to lend helping hands. A bee of neighbours swarmed to help cut a winter's wood supply for a man who cut his arm badly. Another family woke one morning to find their field of grain cradled and stooked. They gasped with surprise and thankfulness, for their neighbours had come in the night and had done what was called a fairy deed—work for a sick neighbour unbeknownst to him and unbidden.

In times of severe flu epidemics, people who remained well went from farm to farm where families lay ill and milked the cows and fed the livestock. Others visited to do a washing, bake bread and generally help out until their neighbours were back on their feet. Older children were often sent to sit up for the night with sick relatives. Chicken soup, onion poultices or mustard plasters were used to bring down fevers with the hope of speedy recoveries.

Neighbourhood corn cuttings and threshings were busy times for the women as well as the men. Early mornings saw the long skirted women putting food and whole sets of dishes into wagons to take to the farm that had the threshing mill or corn cutting that day. It took many hands to get the food ready to feed the hungry crews the noon meal and often the evening one as well.

Neighbours, gathered at community bees, had a chance to socialize and give council to those who were struggling with grief or hard times as well as accomplishing an inordinate amount of farm work. Barn raisings, sawing bees and husking bees often had dances after the work was done. Parlours and newly constructed barn floors bounced and vibrated with dancing feet and fiddle music, while sleeping babes were bundled in a row on a straw tick in the sleeping loft and youngsters sagged into corners when they could take no more excitement.

It was at bees and dances that young laddies met young lassies and began their courting. In the fall, husking bees were discussed with great anticipation. The barns rang with the shouts and songs of the happy hearted youths and maidens and the music of flying corn.

Courting was also done in parlours by the light of a plain tallow dip or in the shadows by a kitchen hearth. If the fire blazed up too brightly, a shovelful of ashes dimmed the light that reached the couple cuddled in a corner. A sure sign of "things turning serious" was if the girl got up and put ashes on the fire as well!

Courting did not always go smoothly. When a young man wished to make a good impression, his horse was not always cooperative. During one Sunday drive a swain's horse spooked as it trotted over a log bridge and the cutter tipped. The two sweethearts landed in the river. As luck would have it the river was frozen so they were only scraped up a bit and not soaked in frigid water.

Many the young couple of courting age knew that driving home in a cutter drawn by a smart stepping horse was exciting where the snow was deepest and the pitch holes numerous. Pitch holes caused occasional upsets and great fun ensued in the soft, deep snow as long as the horse did not take off and leave them stranded. "Such misadventures produced enough merriment to make the young folks forget about the next days turn with the axe in the bush or the scrubbing of pans and kettles or the spinning wheel."[7]

> George Easton's diary of 1838 documents a double wedding. "140 guests bidden and ten fiddlers there." Having a double celebration was very practical when wedding guests travelled on foot from miles around.

Sometimes horses did leave couples stranded after an upset. The tall clock tower in Lanark Village once witnessed a driverless horse and buggy come up the street in the early hours of the morning and turn into its own livery stable. Hours later, a bedraggled, weary and footsore couple came down the street. They had walked all the way from Herron's Mills to Lanark in the dark. Sage advice given to them was "always keep both hands on the lines!"

Life in the pioneering days was not all community celebration and dedication to helping neighbours make a go of their homesteads. The community fabric was more complicated than hard farm work and pious Sunday worship. As early as 1824, traditional religious prejudices and perceived unfairnesses caused major conflict in the area of Morphy's Falls (Carleton Place) and Shipman's Falls (Almonte) in the District of Bathurst.

The earliest Protestant Scottish and Irish settlers believed that new Catholic immigrants from Ireland were receiving a more generous settlement assistance package than they had received. These new immigrants were called the Ballygiblin settlers. Armed conflict, riots and brawls in the countryside ensued after a drinking bout on a Militia Muster day at the Mill Road Tavern, near Morphy's Falls. Shootings, lootings and the burning of log schoolhouses were some of the crimes committed as a result of the extreme ill will that developed after the initial riot.

George Tennant held the office of Magistrate in the District of Bathurst. He had several encounters with the Ballygiblins. Once a number of the ruffians were arrested and bound to oxcarts. When they were brought to him as magistrate, he had them temporarily untied and given food in his own home before they were taken on to gaol in Perth. In spite of his fair dealing with them, he was attacked one day while in Shipman's Falls with a load of grain to be ground. He and the miller had to barricade themselves in the gristmill for protection until the attackers withdrew.

Frequently in those unsettled months, Ballygiblin youths hijacked loads of supplies being hauled from Bytown (Ottawa) by the settlers. On one occasion, they not only stole a man's load but beat him severely and left him lying on his sleigh. His team of horses found their way home with their master unconscious on the sleigh.

Night travel through the dense forest was a difficult and dangerous undertaking for the early pioneers, whether there was turmoil between factions in the community or not. These lines of a poem describe it.

> On journeys after dark we took, to keep wild
> beasts at bay,
> A torch or two of good pitch pine, which also lit
> the way;
> And through the gloomy forest we heard a gaunt
> wolf howl,
> The yawling of a catamount [wildcat] or the
> hooting of an owl,
> When neighbours were in trouble, of course we
> had to go,
> But we did not walk for pleasure [those many years
> ago].[8]

Some warm shards of light were visible in the black of night. The clay and rough mortar chinking between the logs was weakened by the drying and warping of the newly-laid, green logs. Lantern light shone through holes and cracks between the logs of homes nestled in the forest near roadways. A traveller once wrote of these homes shining in the dark of night saying, "When you were outside at night and the fire inside was bright, the shanty bore a striking similitude to a tin lantern."[9] Pierced tin lanterns of the day held candles whose light shone out the pin-hole designs in the metal.

Other light in the night sky came from various forms of commerce. Glowing lights on hillsides, seen bright against the dark sky, came from fired lime kilns. Resinous wood was lit in the kilns under a pile of broken limestone and

Two pioneer candle lanterns, one with glass sides and one of pierced tin through which the candlelight flickered. For many years this tin lantern hung on a peg ready for use in a dark root cellar. CLAUDIA SMITH

the hot fire changed the stones to powder in the course of a few days. Low flames or embers also flared in the blackness of the night where log piles were burning to ash to make potash.

Travel on the roadways of the countryside in the blackness of a moonless night was a tricky business. Good horses easily followed the roads home if they were familiar with the tracks. Other horses seemed to have no sense at all and would wander off the beaten path. One night in a terrible thunderstorm, Joe Tennant was making his way home and the ride was a rough one. Unable to see, he counted on his horse to find the way but instead the horse was stumbling along through stumps with the buggy bumping behind it. Flashes of lightening were all the illumination there was for him to try to drive the horse off the road allowance and back on the road.

The nights of long ago were described as being "as dark as a wolf's mouth" and sometimes people got quite lost in the darkness. One night, Jim W. McIntosh lost his bearings and got out of his rig to find some landmark. He bumped heavily into what he thought was a stump. In frustration, he gave it a kick and it moved away. If new fangled buggy lamps had been available, he might not have had such a close encounter with a large, hairy beast.

In this 1889 advertisement a wily advertiser challenged those who had fast horses to try to pass the powerful lamplight.

The Dietz Driving Lamp
Keeps 200 yards
ahead of your
smartest horse!

Buggy lamps became an essential safety feature of horse transportation once automobiles began to share the roadways. Battery powered lamps were a boon to night travellers and the battery and switch were kept under the buggy or sleigh seat. No longer did travellers have to count on the faint light from houses shining across fields or down laneways to orient themselves as they trotted their horses home after a dance, Scotch concert, church festival or from a Literary Society or prayer meeting.

---

1 William Wye Smith, "Illustrations of Canadian Life," *Rose Belford's Canadian Monthly and National Review*, Vol.8, No.2, (February 1882), p. 160.
2 Ibid., p. 160.
3 Donald McNicol,*The Road To Perth*, Scrapbook, Mrs. J. R. Reid, Courtesy of the Middleville and District Museum.
4 *Historical Sketch of McDonald's Corners, Snow Road and Elphin*, 1875-1995. p. 51.
5 The *Almonte Gazette*, March 27, 1896.
6 Robert Lamond, *A Narrative of the Rise and Progress of Emigration from the Counties of Lanark and Renfrew to the New Settlements of Upper Canada*; (Glasgow, 1821), Canadian Heritage Publications, 1978; p. 91.
7 McNicol, *Ellis's Hill.*
8 Jean Rankin, Scrapbook, Courtesy of the Middleville and District Museum, Anonymous Poem, *Sixty Years Ago*.
9 Edwin C. Guillet, *The Pioneer and Backwoodsman, Volume 1*, (The Ontario Publishing Co. Ltd. 1963), Quoting John Langton, p. 51.

Chapter 6
Hither and Yon

"THE HORSES ran away, going and coming from town" was a terse, 1925, diary entry by Mrs. Milton McKay recounting the dangerous antics of a fractious team. Startled horses took the bits in their teeth and raced uncontrollably down roadways or streets. Neighbours seeing trouble tried to stop teams which careened past their gates, but tragic sudden death or injury from being thrown out of a buggy or sleigh during a runaway was not uncommon. Trampled bystanders, wrecked wagons and broken wheels and harness were other consequences of horses out of control. Oncoming trains and automobiles as well as dogs, horseflies and even shadows in ditches were enough to startle horses into bolting.

An upset wagon caused the death of Archie Campbell as he headed home from Caldwell's Mill, in Lanark, with a load of grain. His horses were frightened by something and started to run. As they gathered speed, one wagon wheel hit a rock and upset the load crushing him under a pile of fallen sacks of grain. The spot was marked by three notches chopped into a picket of the roadside rail fence. The marks remained as a memorial for many years.

Late 1800s Fly Help For Horses:
Take three handfuls of walnut leaves and add boiling water, 1 pint per handful. Let walnut tea cool and bottle it off. Before the horse goes out, damp his ears and other parts most troubled with the infusion with a sponge.

Sunday driving on a golden June day in 1888, proved dangerous for two young Clayton ladies out in their buggy for a pleasant jaunt. The horse took fright and threw Misses Banning and O'Neil to the ground. Thankfully neither was seriously injured and bystanders caught the spooked young horse. A newspaper reported the accident under the descriptive headline: "A Sudden Horizontalization."

Just at dusk, after the Perth Fair of 1907, a couple was driving home at a merry trot when an oncoming train startled their horse into a burst of speed that became uncontrollable. The racing rig rounded a turn by an old toll-gate and the whole outfit upset. The occupants were hurled to the ground and the horse hightailed it toward home, along the road to Balderson. The frightened animal with the remains of the buggy bouncing at its terrified heels was caught near the Balderson Cheese Factory.

One winter day, a fellow from the back country started for Lanark with a load of cordwood. He left his team standing for a few minutes while he stopped at Jackson Willows on an errand. In his absence, the horses became frightened and ran wildly down the road toward Ferguson's Falls, scattering blocks of wood along the way. The whole sleighload capsized and the horses continued running until they collided with a gatepost. The neighbour drove the stranded man to find his team and sleigh and many helpful hands turned out to help reload the wood.

Horses loose on the roads were not always there by accident. Some children rode old work horses to school. With the reins tied over their necks, the horses were sent back along the road home with a slap on the rump. The homing instincts of another horse were used in a different way. As a youngster, Alice McIntosh enjoyed visiting at a neighbour's on winter afternoons. When it was time to come home her father hitched up their horse to the cutter

Two advertisements in the *Canadian Countryman* of the 1920s that offered help to farm families with unruly horses.

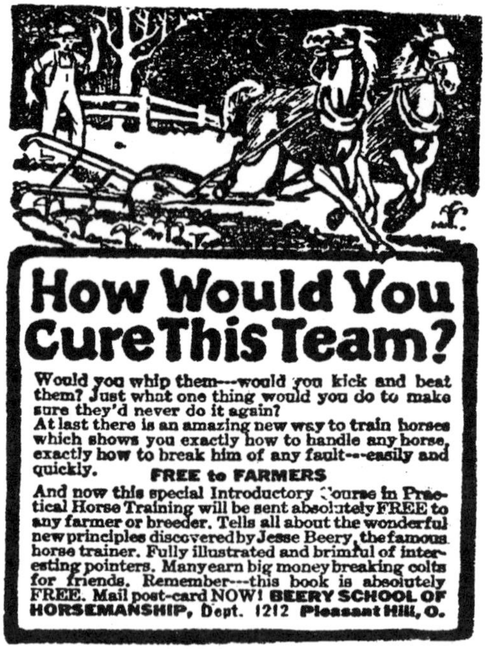

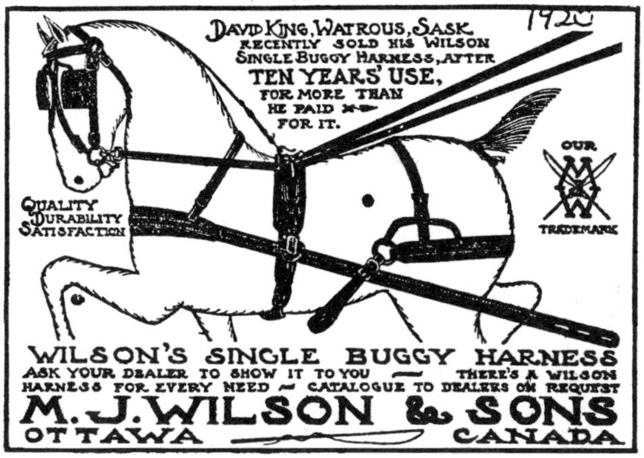

Top quality, strong harness was necessary for farm and road work. Local harness makers were kept busy. As well, people could order harness from advertisements in newspapers.

and let it go. The horse had been bought from the farm where the girl was visiting, so it trotted straight back to its old home. Alice then jumped into the cutter and drove home.

The story of old Fan was long marvelled at and passed down through the generations. She was a faithful, reliable driving horse that was shared between the families of two Graham brothers. Fan was hitched up whenever one of the families needed to get to town more swiftly than was possible with the heavy team. In the late years of her life, Fan was kept at only one farm. One day, the girls of the other family were delighted to notice Fan walking up their lane unaccompanied. The old mare plodded over to the log house and stuck her head in the open window. The girls scratched her ears and gave her an apple. She soon turned away and returned to her other family, where she lay down and died later that evening.

Neighbours were well aware of each others weaknesses and foibles. When a team was seen weaving down the road or walking in the wrong track with the driver slouched or lolling in his seat, people knew that drink was the cause. If the wagon was loaded with sacks of grain, they sent the horses on down the mill road. If the wagon was empty, they pointed the horses on the road towards home.

On dark, moonless nights a horse's homing instinct could be helpful. However, one night a group of young people at Union Hall near Clayton thought differently. Due to a difference of opinion as to who would drive which young lady home after a dance, a horse was left untethered by the front door. It decided to go home alone and when the young people came out, their transportation had left. They had to trudge the miles home in the cold and found the horse standing patiently by the stable door having damaged nothing in its driverless trip home.

Bakery wagon horses were involved in an accident in Franktown in 1889. Mr. McBeth's team became startled when the axle broke on the bread wagon. They raced madly down the road tearing up their harness and themselves considerably. The baker was glad the accident had not happened with his spanking new bread wagon that was nearly ready to go into service.

Road accidents happened if poor care was taken of the carts, wagons, buggies and sleighs. Atmospheric conditions weakened the wood of the wheels of all running gear and they deteriorated into a dangerous state. Moisture swelled the spokes in wet weather causing the

A farm family wagon ready to begin a busy day in 1913. COURTESY OF MRS. J.R. REID & THE MIDDLEVILLE AND DISTRICT MUSEUM

springing of the spokes and the splitting of the hubs. Long exposure to sun caused shrinkage of the wood that opened the joints to moisture. Carriages and buggies driven on stony roadways needed painting and varnishing once a year to maintain their strength and good appearance. The frequent painting of farm wagons and sleighs saved many dollars of burdensome expense.

The travelling public used shallow fording places across streams as part of vehicle maintenance. Rough bridges spanned the watercourses where natural gravel fords, or stoned or sunken log fording places were part of the original road. Often teamsters bypassed the bridges and drove their teams through the water at the fords so that the wooden rims of the wheels got a thorough soaking. The creaking spokes, loosened by the dry, dusty roadways, tightened up in the water and thirsty horses were given a chance to take a cool drink from the stream.

Pioneering families, hard at work on their land, did not always have time to check to see if they had any precious missives from the homeland. Outside the post offices, lists were

Mr. William McEwen's horse-drawn mail coach or stage. In 1918 Mr. McEwen substituted gas for horsepower which afforded his passengers faster service and brought him home much earlier.
COURTESY OF THE MIDDLEVILLE AND DISTRICT MUSEUM

posted with the names of anyone receiving mail. Settlers, in town for their supplies, read down the list and picked up any mail for their district and took it along to deliver to their neighbours. In 1859, the post office in Carleton Place ran an advertisement in the *Herald* listing the names of thirty-three people who had unclaimed letters.

Years later when postal deliveries were made to villages, families marked the time by the arrival of the post. In many places, the approach of the mail stage was announced by the sound of a "postal horn" which echoed over the fields and forests. As the horses trotted toward the towns and villages, the mail driver blew "on a large horn from whose flaring mouth the most blatent sounds issued."[1]

Folks of all ages went for the mail with an air of expectancy. While the post master and his assistants deftly sorted the mail, people stood in line hoping to hear from a far away spouse, child, parent or sweetheart. When the wicket clicked open, the throng moved slowly forward to give name or number and then turned away happily clutching a stiff, thick envelope or with shoulders slumped with disappointment.

Mail workers picked up locked mail bags from the village post offices and carried them on foot, on horseback or in a stage wagon to smaller post offices in the countryside. Children were often delegated to run to pick up the mail at the rural postal points or they picked up the family mail as they walked home from school.

The ever faithful mail driver, Mr. Rodgers on the Middleville, Clydesville, Lanark route in

1896, was praised by the *Lanark Era* for his reliability on spring roadways. "He has quite a round-about circuit to make due to washouts and bridges out but he plunges his worthy steeds into the pool or rattles over the stony track in order to "get there" while he spares no pains to make his passengers as comfortable as possible."

With the beginning of rural mail delivery to individual homes around 1908, the stentor call of the postal horn over the fields passed into history. Then time was marked for many rural dwellers each day as they heard the sound of the mail box lid snap shut if their farm was close to the road or perhaps by the bark of their dog as the mail carrier passed. The convenience of the rural mail delivery to the far flung farming families was inestimable. No longer did time consuming trips to town have to be made to pick up the mail when there was field work to be done.

It was essential that the rural mail carriers kept their running gear in a reliable and safe condition for the miles of travelling in the mud and the dust and the snow. Their buggies and sleighs had to be well maintained to get the job done and the mail carriers' horses had to be in fine, sound condition too. Travelling steadily from one farm to the next the horses became very familiar with their daily routine. They stopped at each mailbox along the route and without guidance from their driver, then moved ahead as the lid snapped or squeaked closed.

Some friendly mail drivers took money from the anxious hands of school children. Coins were drawn from deep in pants pockets for the mail driver to buy licorice sticks, peppermints, sawlogs, horehound candies and other sweets from a village store. The next day the children would meet the driver outside the school gate to get their treats.

The mail drivers were also instruments of romance for lovelorn country swains. Notes that a dance was being held at a certain home or hall that night were sent with drivers, who gave assurances that the messages would be delivered promptly. Rendezvous points were set up and sometimes a double date was requested with a younger sister. Sighs and secret smiles punctuated the day of farm chores with such notes in the wind.

House parties were popular forms of entertainment in both summer and winter. To make room for the dancers often the furniture had to be moved outside and covered up against the weather. Then, with the rugs rolled back, the square sets formed and the mad fiddle music began. Often the young people kept the festivities going until broad daylight.

There was a lot of horse racing in days past and the competition was fierce along the roads. After a party or dance, young people often rose to the challenge to race home. Late one night, after a dance, a fellow harnessed up and trotted off quickly only to turn into a nearby laneway to hide. His challenger went speeding past and must have torn along the road home wondering just how fast his friend's horse could be.

Young Jack Rankin's horse had a habit of coming up behind a buggy or sleigh on the open road. If it was not allowed to pass, it kept pace with its head hanging in between the two passengers in the vehicle in front.

Rules of the Road

An Ontario statute of 1873 regulated the driving and riding of horses and other animals on highways and public bridges for preventing racing, immoderate or dangerous driving. Signs were posted on many bridges to remind travellers of the speed limit on the bridges.

A statute of 1877 decreed, No person shall race with, or drive furiously any horse or other animal or shout or use blasphemous or indecent language upon any highway.

The travelling public did have rules of the road to follow. However, they were often ignored. One hot August night, a couple of young blades with obviously nothing better to do, turned the streets of Smiths Falls into a trotting course. They raced their horses utterly regardless of the rights of the rest of the town. The drunken parties were later summoned before the magistrate for dangerous driving on the public roads.

Every fall gangs of forest workers from villages and farms headed to the "timber limits" of virgin forests. For these loggers and shantymen, "stopping places" along the roads to the timber limits were essential. The gangs needed places to stay at night as they drove their ponderous teams along. With more and more teams joining in on the way, larger and

Alec Schoular, Madge Creighton and Nettie off for a Sunday drive or to a picnic. PA-77239

larger places were needed to accommodate the men and their horses, the closer they got to the cutting front.

In Dalhousie Township, near Poland, the large Duncan McIntosh farmhouse was an important stopping place for loggers. Anne McIntosh provided meals, beds and whiskey, as well as fodder for their horses. Another popular stopping place in the mid 1800s, was the Sneddon's Rosebank Inn near Blakeney. As many as "twenty span" or forty horses were tied in their stable on a single night, when the shantymen were heading up the Ottawa Valley for a winter of bush work.

For the convenience of the travelling public, as well as the shantymen, licensed taverns were sprinkled along the major roads and were required to furnish good clean beds and palatable "victuals" to travellers together with hay and grain for the accommodation of their beasts. The yeomen from the back townships spent long, thirsty hours on the roads transporting their loads of logs, grain or other produce to town and picking up supplies. These groups staunchly supported the renewal of tavern licences for "Houses of Entertainment" along their routes. They vouched for the innkeepers, swearing on petitions that each innkeeper was a fit and proper person to hold a tavern ticence, thus ensuring that their stopping places stayed open for their convenient patronage.

Women rarely frequented such places and did not find these establishments a boon to their existence. The temptation for a wee drop overcame many men as they neared each stopping place. When accompanying their husbands to town, the women were often left outside these taverns in the freezing cold to hold the horses or to sit shivering in the sleigh. One can imagine that as the couple travelled along, the atmosphere in the sleigh must have been frostier than the weather.

Liquor proved to be a deadly problem for a pioneer who took a load of potash to Perth. On the way home, he tied his team up in front of a stopping place in Ferguson's Falls while he took some liquid refreshment. When he resumed the trip, he overlooked the fact that he had taken the bits out of the horses' mouths at the tavern. Without this control over his team, they could not be stopped when they began to run as they neared home. Neighbours ran to his aid when the sleigh plunged over a small bridge. Calming his horses and moving the poor man out of the snowy bog was all they were able to do. The man was fatally injured and when asked if he wanted a priest, the unfortunate fellow said, "No, just take me home to my wife and family."

The problems that liquor caused in families and within communities, were major concerns in the pioneer days. A group of men met in St. Andrew's Hall, in Dalhousie Township, to form a Temperance Society, as early as 1831. Summer evenings saw men treading the paths out of the bush and along the stony roads to the hall to discuss temperance and the evil of drink. George Easton reflected in his diary that, "Nothing is talked of but moralizing the Curly maple and the knotty hemlock - - or rather the drunken blackguards in the wilds of Dalhousie. The love of whiskey it seems is our besetting sin . . ."

Temperance Society meetings were eagerly attended by young people in the late 1800s. Called the Band of Hope, then the Loyal Crusaders and later the Cadets of Temperance, the group was well supported, not only for uplifting, moral guidance but for a chance to get out and meet other young people. At age fourteen, young people joined the Sons of Temperance. Hopes were high that children would adhere to their pledge of sobriety when they became adults.

New Year's festivities involved an intensive sharing of liquor. "Ne'ar Day" celebrations were held in town halls everywhere and the "eight-hand reel," a favourite dance from the old country was a central part of the fun. Long after much of the "Glesca" accent had faded from the settlers' tongues, the Scotch custom of "first footing" was retained. It involved trooping around to neighbours' homes before daylight, lustily proclaiming, "A guid New Year tae ane and a'." Black, shiny bottles were produced from pockets to share a "wee tait" to celebrate. This custom was abhorred by many and praise was given as the tradition faded into history.

In 1909 a local news item noted, "The old time custom of visiting neighbours with a whiskey bottle before daylight, passed away long ago and may it never return." New Year celebrations continued in a more moderate way. In Elphin, a tea meeting was held on New Year's night, in 1909, at the Presbyterian church. Even nature put forth her best efforts by furnishing beautiful moonlight and perfect sleighing, making it an ideal night for driving. Many from a distance took advantage of it.

In the early 1900s, a referendum on prohibition was a hot topic. Before voting day, church groups and temperance organizations were whipping the character of Lanarkites into a "thick moral cream." People flocked to the Lanark County Temperance Association meetings, held in every hamlet and village, to listen to exhortations on the issue. Model Ts and horse drawn vehicles shared the roads and headed for the meeting halls, probably heckled along the way by those of a contrary mind.

---

1 C.M. Forbes, "History Of Lanark Village Covers An Eighty-Five Year Period," The *Perth Courier*, February 2, 1906.

CHAPTER 7
The Art of Neighbouring

ROAD conditions in the late fall and early spring were always touch and go. Choosing between wheels and runners for a trip to town or church was often a difficult guessing game as the seasons exchanged earth for snowdrifts or packed sleigh tracks to mud and ruts.

When wheels did give way to runners for winter travel, the constant traffic on the roads slowed down only slightly. With lofts, bins and cellar shelves full, Old Man Winter didn't scare anyone. The frigid winter temperatures and drifted country roads did not keep the hardy yeomen and their families at home by their hearths. Bulky buffalo robes were shaken out for winter sleighing after being layered in cedar all summer in air tight barrels. Bundled under the buffaloes and with sleigh bells ringing, the families went to town for supplies or to church every Sunday.

Lieutenant J.C. Morgan wrote an emigrant's guide book in 1824. His description of the settlers in the new world enjoying a certain portion of recreation and pleasure during the winter included these details, ". . . Excepting those who had newly taken possession of their lands and whose every day was precious . . . sleighs were prepared for visiting neighbours and friends probably many miles distant. The careful house-wife then begins to anticipate a holiday, and once more wrapped in her best bear-skin cloak, surmounted by a fur bonnet large and ugly enough for half a dozen people, she shines forth in all her glory, ready and willing to share in all the pleasures of her lord."[1]

Snow padded hooves and whispering sleigh runners made very little noise in the snow as the horses trotted along. Silent runners were a menace to other sleighs and pedestrians so sleighbells were hung on sleigh shafts and rang out merrily to signal the approach of sleighs. To prevent collisions, an 1855 Ontario statute decreed that, "any person travelling upon any highway with a sleigh, sled or cariole

You must be a Jingler of the Bells,
If you want to go to Lanark in a Sleigh.

Our Village Council have sat in solemn deliberation, and the decree has come forth that

EVERY ONE
MUST WEAR BELLS.

A load of wood went over a boy on the street, with terrible results. The load was upset and the wood scattered — neither had Bells on. The boy said he didn't mind a few scratches; that his back was itchey any way.

The best place to buy these indispensible Jingle Bells is at

Moran's Harness Shop.

Whips, Blankets, Rugs, Etc., Etc.

SINGLE DOUBLE COURSE FINE HARNESS
IN GREAT VARIETY.

☞ Give us a call,

JOHN MORAN,
LANARK, ONT.

A Lanark Village harness maker took advantage of a new Council decree that bells were mandatory for safety in the village with an advertisement in the *Lanark Era*, 1896.

drawn by a horse or by a mule shall have at least two bells attached to the harness."

Sleigh bells came in many sizes, shapes and musical tones. Every neighbour's bells had a different sound so often people knew who was coming around the curve in the road before they saw them. There were backpad bells, shaft bells consisting of three small bells on each shaft, and turkey bells that hung from the martingales at the chests of the heavy horses. At every step and with each toss of the head the bells jingled and the happy sound was a welcome, glad part of the winter months.

The children in the Thompson family always knew when their grandfather was coming. Their keen ears caught the sound of his "round about bells," a string of bells on a leather strap that buckled around his horse and fastened to the backpad. These bells had the

Thomas McKay on his way to town for groceries or off to church on a snowy morning with a set of "round about bells" on his driving horse. PA-79163

best sound and could be heard the farthest over the snowy roadways.

The country roadways drifted in solidly in the wild snows and wind of a blizzard. Often fields blew clear. Bad blood leading to a feud could spring up if one neighbour denied another access to a field, when the road was plugged with drifts of snow. One teamster requested the right to cross on an easier path through the field and was denied with the excuse that his horses' droppings would leave too many weed seeds. Frustration and rage sprang into the farmer's breast and the slight was not easily put aside in their future dealings over the years.

1864 was a harrowing year of frigid temperatures and deep snows. The Caldwell Company of Lanark sent a gang of woodsmen to the Black River on the east side of the Ottawa River. Thomas Grier and the gang, travelling with the four yokes of oxen and three teams of horses, set out from the Maberly area. The eleven-day trek via Clayton, Pakenham and on to Sand Point and Fort Coulonge on the Quebec side of the river was a gruelling one for the men and beasts. They found themselves bogged down in snow seven feet deep in places. Their food supplies and energy reserves ran dangerously low on the trip. All the roads of the countryside were blocked and supplies were scarce for farming families too who were trapped on their farms during the weeks of snow.

Winter road maintenance was a neighbourhood affair. Neighbours worked with their horses, shovels and harrows and the township financed snow scrapers for sections of the roads under the direction of their pathmaster. Long hours were spent on the roads after a blizzard, but the results were rough and tunnel-like when the high snow drifts were wind packed. A 1908 road report in the *Lanark Era* told of a storm that "piled billows of the white stuff in all the main roads. Heroic shovelling has cleared the highways and the mails are running but all the back roads are sealed."

It was not until the 1930s that many townships purchased heavy horsedrawn snowplows. This was a big help to the pathmasters (now being called patrolmen). Clearing the snow was a job that worked up a steaming, white lather on the farm teams. In a light snow, the plow took two teams, one hitched on the front and one behind on a push pole. After a heavy storm, two or three teams pulled and one pushed. Sometimes up to six teams were needed and they would get so played out that no headway could be made at all. Then a fresh team was put on the front to continue the exhausting task of breaking the trail.

Good use was made of ice roads across lakes or rivers to shorten the miles to town, when winter's cold grip on the water made the passage safe. Such a lake road was used every winter between Galbraith and Clayton. Loads of cord wood, grain and logs for the sawmill were hauled over the ice road. Young people took the road to go to dances in Clayton. The trip home was always made with the heavy buffalo robes pulled over their heads, while the horses went along unguided, knowing exactly where their warm stalls were.

Sometimes mid-winter weather conditions made ice roads almost impassable for weeks, due to deep slush on the ice. The residents complained of the messy travelling but the ice roads were still convenient shortcuts. These roads could be very unreliable as spring came on. A terrible tragedy happened to a family using the road across Robb's Lake near Tatlock. Returning home one night by sleigh, the entire family, children and all were lost in the bitterly cold waters under the ice. The complete disappearance of the family was a deep shock to the whole community.

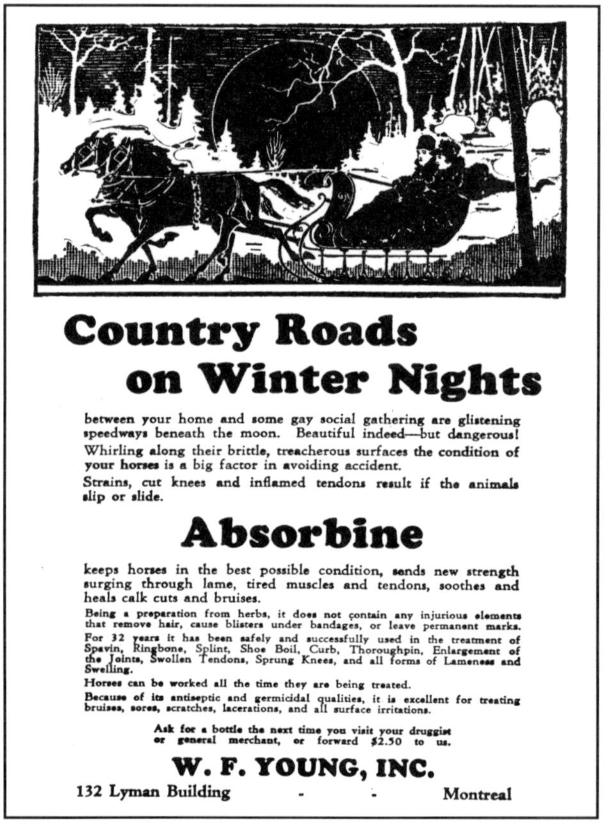

An advertisement for the horseman's standby – Absorbine – a liniment for sore muscles and tendons. Circa 1920.

The date when people got out their sleighs and buffalo robes depended on "the forwardness of winter." Usually the roads were snow covered and sleighs were out of summer storage sheds by the time of the school Christmas concerts. With bells ringing brightly, the families headed down the snow-packed roads of their districts to little one-room school houses. Children, with cheeks rosy from the cold night air and excitement, hurried around their school rooms in last minute preparations for their pageants, recitations and music drills, while their parents threw blankets over their horses' broad backs against the winter's cold and tied them to the schoolyard fence. Amid much snowy feet stamping and calls of greetings among neighbours, the adults entered the schools with plates of food and settled onto boards, set on blocks of wood, to enjoy the concert.

Traipsing snow clogged concession lines in the deep mid-winter to get to school after a blizzard was a tiring ordeal for children. Sleigh tracks were helpful but the easiest one to walk in was the track made by a low slung, wooden jumper sleigh. If the road had not been opened at all, a farmer trailed a log down the road behind a horse, so that his youngsters and neighbour children along the way could follow in the trough made in the snow. Often little children had to step in the footprints of their older brothers and sisters, as they made their way to school where the warmth of a wood stove welcomed them. The stove belched out heat that roasted the scholars sitting in desks nearby and left those sitting farther away to shiver.

In 1851 the children at S.S.#10 Penman's, later the Galbraith School, struggled to school through the drifts and cold, but had no heat whatsoever when they got there each day. The teacher petitioned the trustees of the school section saying "the school house is extraordinarily cold and unfit to be occupied without a stove." The trustees responded to the complaint and all the subscribers came to a meeting at the school house. Horses snorted and stamped along the length of school fence as they waited. The long debate went on into the night as finances were considered. Finally assent was given to buy a stove for £2, 1*s*, 6*d* from Messrs. J.O.F. Heale in Lanark. The stove was delivered by sleigh and the children benefited from the warmth for years and years of study.

Teachers had to deal with scholars shivering with cold after their long walks to school. Children, bundled up for the winter months, presented other problems too. One day, a teacher had to send a little one home for a very necessary bath. The child returned to school presently with a note pinned to his coat that said, "My Joe's no rose. Teach him. Don't smell him."

Poultry fairs were held in many communities in late November and December. Farmers slaughtered their chickens, turkeys and geese and the cold weather of early winter kept the meat cold and fresh for the fairs. Wagons or sleighs loaded with dressed fowl were driven along the iron hard roadways to the poultry fairs all over the county. The purchases of winter provisions and Christmas items depended directly on the prices paid by the buyers who came from large centres to purchase poultry to resell in the towns.

The poultry fair in Almonte was a big affair which attracted American buyers. Farm families were encouraged to bring their birds to the fair "well fatted."
ALMONTE GAZETTE, 1885

At the Almonte Poultry Fair of 1919, eight tons of turkeys and geese were purchased. The highest price received was nine cents a pound.

In the old days, Christmas visits with relations involved yoking up the team of oxen to a low sleigh and driving many miles along snowy roadways. Children were bundled into a box, especially affixed to the sleigh. Well-covered with quilts and with a heated flat rock or two tucked under the blankets, the children stayed cozy for the trip. The adults sat exposed to the elements, protected only by heavy goat skin or buffalo robes that cut the bite of the wind as they travelled.

When they reached their destination and turned in the familiar laneway, strains of fiddle music floated out over the frosty air. The open arms of family and the smell of goose, bread, plum pudding, and fruit pies welcomed them. The children darted for the big, open fireplace to warm their chilled toes and happily cracked hickory nuts or black walnuts with their cousins. For New Year's, families often reversed the trips and the Christmas host and hostess got all togged up and did the travelling for the celebrations.

Shooting matches were held during the Christmas and New Year's season and crack shots travelled all around the countryside to compete. Winter road conditions or brisk, frosty weather did not deter sharpshooters from far flung communities such as Flower Station, Poland, Clayton and Perth from patronizing a shooting match in Brightside in December, 1895. The *Lanark Era* reported, "There were twenty rounds fired in all and the spoil was well divided as each of the competitors carried away turkeys and geese enough for a good Christmas feed."

When snowy winter weather made good sleighing, huge loads were transported along the roadways. In 1909, there was a report of an immense load of phosphate drawn to Perth from a mine near Otty Lake. "The load weighed five tons all but 250 pounds."[2] Horses also strained in their collars to move loads of ice to cheese factories and stores. Blocks 18" x 18" or 24" x 24", were cut out of rivers and lakes with ice saws. The cakes of ice were bounced in the water with ice tongs to heave them up out of the hole. The force of the water helped lift the heavy blocks and then they were levered onto sleighs or teams of horses pulled them up ramps and onto sleighs.

February was the month to concentrate on cutting the summer supply of ice for households too. Many farmers "took time by the forelock" and worked at filling their ice houses and packing the big, clear ice cakes in sawdust. Farm families needed a supply of ice for the summer in order to keep Saturday night's and Sunday's milk cool until Monday morning, when the cheese factory opened again. On some farms, the factory cans were kept in a cool milkhouse with a smaller creamery can, partly filled with ice, set in the milk. Milk cans were also set in tubs of ice water to keep the milk fresh. Cheesemakers kicked if sour milk was poured into their vats on Mondays, as it lowered the quality of the cheese.

> From the Mississippi district came the report that the people of "that vicinity have completed the harvesting of their ice. A good supply has been laid in for the summer."
>
> *Lanark Era*, March 6, 1918.

People also took advantage of snowy roads to sleigh-haul heavy loads of grain to the grist mills. In December 1885, the Caldwells exchanged their grain grinding burr stones for a new roller system in the village of Lanark. This wise business decision was based on the fact that although the men brought the grain to the mill, it was really the women who were the customers. The efficient new mill produced a fine flour that satisfied the ladies so the miller had no fear for their continued patronage. Sleigh loads of grain were driven from many corners of Lanark by request of housewives wanting the smooth, fine flour for baking.

> In 1877, an Ontario statute allowed county councils to pass a bylaw to make double tracks during the season of sleighing, so that teams would be able to pass without being obliged to turn out when meeting each other.

Winter conditions and clear weather usually made travelling smooth and speedy. People took the opportunity to make long trips to visit relatives. A February entry in Joseph Tennant's 1887 diary mentions a journey from the Almonte area but storms dogged the trip. "Started on a visit to the Front [along the St. Lawrence River] with Uncle Joe. Away for six days. Had very bad roads."

Days of bright sleighing and evenings of moonlit beauty were other aspects of winter travel. Stopping the team to look out over a grove of snow-laden pines washed in moonlight made the dreadful blizzard conditions, of perhaps only a week ago, fade into the background of memory. Families would call out, "The sleighing is capital tonight!" as they passed each other on the road. Gay laughter also rang out when groups of young people were driving home from a Literary Society meeting or party. Sometimes, if the driver was a prankster, he arranged to pull the draw bolt that held the horses to the sleigh, and the whole party landed in the snow drifts.

Between forty and fifty young people of a Mission Band and church choir were invited to a party one winter night in 1918. The journey between town and farm was made in wide open sleighs that allowed for "a panoramic view of the Aurora Borealis that flitted and streamed, illuminating the heavens like an army of search-lights. The sleighs were loaded to capacity, if not overloaded, on account of the numbers of feet hanging over the gunwale, port and star-board and swept the snow billows as these huge snow ships sailed along. The way was safely navigated by the teamsters who negotiated the swells and shoals and brought their human cargo intact into the harbour of the host farm."[3]

One afternoon, some young people from Almonte, in search of entertainment, piled into a sleigh pulled by a four-horse team. They were curling enthusiasts and set out for Lanark where they curled a few rocks on an outdoor rink with the curlers from the village and stayed the night. The next day they went on to Perth and curled some more. With their brooms and boots piled into the sleigh they made their way home via Carleton Place where they again curled several ends.

A long toboggan slide at Perth was the site of many winter fêtes lit by flickering lantern light. Special races with prizes were organized and some evenings there was even a band in attendance. The 42nd Band of Smiths Falls bundled into sleighs and went to Perth to entertain big crowds one drizzly night. Everyone enjoyed the coasting and the music despite the misty rain. Ladies' races were a big attraction as well as races for "toboggans with runners" and "toboggans without."

The art of neighbouring was a strong component of country communities in good times and bad. In the summer months, dust swirling from under horses' feet and rolling out behind the buggy wheels meant trouble. Someone "raising a stour" or a trail of dust indicated the approach of a doctor or a person in need of help. Neighbours were always ready to lend a hand, be it searching for a lost child, rescuing a horse down a well, quelling a house or barn fire or helping at a logging accident.

Winter conditions hampered emergency situations. "Operation Snowplow" was a neighbourhood effort to get a sick man to hospital after a blizzard. The teams were "bogged" through and shovels were used when the steaming animals could plunge no further. All the while, the patient lay bundled on a mattress on a waiting sleigh, while the lathered teams ahead broke the trail. The track was not smooth and the sleigh jerked and pitched with the movements of the straining horses, much to the discomfort of the suffering man. It took all night to fight through the snow but finally the doctor was able to get through from his end

A postcard of an old-time doctor on his way to the bedside of an injured or ill patient.
COURTESY OF THE MIDDLEVILLE AND DISTRICT MUSEUM

and meet them on the road. He made the fellow more comfortable and then they took him on to the hospital. There is an old saying that "You can get along without your friends but you can't get along without your neighbours." This man appreciated the truth of that wisdom that cold winter's night.

Hastily hitched horses were urged to a fast pace one winter day when a young McIntyre lad, moaning in pain, was swathed in blankets to be rushed to the hospital in Almonte. The horses trotted out smartly and neighbours helped keep the child still and warm as he lay in the long sleigh box, but it was too late. The child died in the sleigh before they could reach the hospital. His appendix had ruptured.

Winter or summer, in all sorts of weather country doctors hastened to stricken patients around their districts. Often livery stable horses and rigs were hired to make house calls. When the doctor got back to town, the livery proprietor had another horse harnessed, ready and waiting to go. In the winter, the long, cold drives to see patients in the back country were an ordeal of perseverance and dedication.

Whenever the skills of a practical nurse were needed to assist the doctor, he would just arrive at their doors. These hardy and dedicated women would jump right into the sleigh and go off to help any family in need. Other women gave great service to the community as midwives. Bessie McIntyre remembers that as a child she often woke in the morning to find that her mother, Rachel Manson, had been called out during the night. When she asked where her mother was, her Dad would say, "Oh, she's away to a huskin'." Thick knitted mitts, honey, grain or other farm produce were given as payment for helping with the birth of a child.

On more tragic occasions, women died in childbirth or their wee babes died within short days of birth. The graveyards of Lanark County are stark witness to lost young female lives. There is an old saying that reveals unspeakable travail, desperation and sorrow. The pioneer reality often was, "It took a man three wives to raise a family."

In the very early days of settlement, Lieutenant Morgan reported on life in the colony of Canada. In 1824, he wrote, "I must not forget to notice the great scarcity of medical men throughout Upper Canada. It is no uncommon thing to see an MD making a journey of thirty or forty miles to inquire after the health of his patients, with his cutting and carving apparatus with the contents of a small chemist's shop crammed into a leathern bag, banging away upon the ribs of his favourite [horse]."[4] It was not until many years later that Lanark County could boast the services of travelling doctors.

The distances to procure medical help were vast and "sometimes the cost of inadequate transportation had to be paid in human life. If the nearest doctor was a forty-mile walk away, a man could be excused for hesitating before summoning help - and by the time he did act, it might be too late. Many people who fell ill in pioneer [days] died before a doctor could reach them."[5]

Children who suffered terrible burns when a lantern was pulled over by tiny hands, or youngsters kicked or stepped on by horses or cattle, all needed medical attention. The first child buried in the Rosetta Cemetery fell into a potash kettle. Little Johnny Croft of Middleville tumbled into a large soap making pot and died. Other children wheezed and choked with whooping cough or sickened with diphtheria. Medical help could do little for them and desperate parents were left to mourn and erect simple crosses or plank headstones.

A plank grave marker put in place on the deaths of "2 Children, Dear Boys, V.M. King, 1866-1872, 2 Boys, Come Onto Me All Little Children." CLAUDIA SMITH

Wise women with the knowledge of soothing or healing herbs were often consulted in the absence of trained medical doctors. Tonics, poultices, syrups and salves, made by women who had backwoods wisdom, eased the lives of the settlers. However they could not cure everything and doctors were needed.

With the installation of the telephone service around the turn of the century, no longer did distressed neighbours or desperate relations have to make a mad dash on horseback or behind a galloping farm team to fetch the doctor for an accident victim or in the case of extreme illness. If an emergency arose,

Cold weather ailment remedies for horses were advertised in 1914.

the doctor's office tried to contact him on a rural phone line. The receptionist or "hello girl" at "central" was contacted in the vicinity of his last known case and families were alerted to watch for him and flag him down as he went by on the road. The message of where he was needed next was passed on and the conscientious medical man would be off at great speed with packed snowballs from his horse's flying hooves pelting the sleigh dashboard as they travelled along.

Everyone travelling with horses in the winter had the snowball problem on mild days. Moist snow packed and balled up under horses' hooves very readily. The hard snowballs, sometimes four inches high made walking difficult for the horses and would break away unevenly leaving the horse with one hoof balled up and another not. Stumbling and leg strain

The road in summer that passed the Middleville S.S.#6 school with the cheese factory on the right. PA-79041

was a real danger. When pulling a heavy load of wood uphill, horses with packed hooves could not get a good grip on the road so teamsters carried a balling hammer hooked to the harness collar. It had a sharp point and was used to knock off the snowballs before a long draw up a hill. Horseshoes with bevelled inside edges were also used to prevent this persistent, time wasting problem.

The road past the Middleville school from Anderson's Rapids in the winter. Many loads of shingles, lumber and barrels were teamed out along the road from the Clyde Mill owned by J.W. Anderson and his sons. PA-79044

The length of the sleighing season each year depended on the "backwardness of spring." Choosing between wheels and runners when moving house in the early spring was a tricky business.

A family who chose runners for a March moving day found out that spring was not backward that year. When the day began there was good sleighing with six inches of fresh snow. Neighbours drove three teams of horses with sleighs to help transport the furniture and household goods. However, with a shift of the wind and rising temperatures, the snow began to melt and by noon the sleighing was gone.

When the loaded sleighs were only half-way to the new home the road was nearly bare earth. The sleigh runners scratched and lurched from one last snowy patch to another. The three teams were reined in through a nearby farm gate. A request was made for a place to leave the sleighs and large barn doors were opened to provide a storage space until wagons could be fetched to complete the move.

Maple syrup was marketed in the spring. Many milk cans of the amber liquid were delivered to towns and villages and peddled door to door from the backs of sleighs, wagons or Model T Fords. The syrup was ladled into crocks, cans, and honey pails in whatever quantities the customers wanted to buy.

One year early spring weather presented a problem for Maynard and Blanche McIntosh. On a bright, spring day they set out for Almonte with several milk cans full of syrup set safely in their double sleigh. There was fresh snow on the ground and it seemed like a fine morning for travelling. Half-way to town there was no snow left. They had to drive the sleigh scratching along the dirt road and all through town.

Milk cans full of sweet maple syrup in the back of a 1913 Model T Ford on the road to market.
COURTESY OF DONALD AND MARION DODDS

Much as we rely on traffic and road condition reports today, the state of the roads was always highlighted in community news columns long ago. In 1895, warm weather returned for Christmas travel and a road report said, "Alas, our good sleighing has all disappeared and the roads are in as good a slush as mud and water can make them." In the *Lanark Era* of March 13, 1918 there was a comment, "Today makes one hundred and eleven [days] of sleighing in Lanark."

The *Perth Courier* reported on March 18, 1898, "The robin has returned and welcome beautiful spring. The jingle of sleigh bells is heard no more as the snow has disappeared and the buggies are brought out." The Clayton news in the *Almonte Gazette* of March 19, 1920 noted, "The snow is almost gone - Wagons and buggies are the only conveyances now. Wheels went through to Almonte and Carleton Place on Friday for the first time this year." As the frost came out of the ground and springs bubbled up on roadways to form bogs some community reports very simply stated, "The roads are pretty bad just now."

---

1 Lieutenant J. C. Morgan H P., *The Emigrant's Notebook and Guide with Recollections of Upper and Lower Canada During the Late War*, (London, 1824), p.286.
2 The *Perth Courier*, February 5, 1909.
3 The *Lanark Era*. February, 1918.
4 Morgan, *Emigrant's Notebook*, p.280.
5 Edwin C. Guillet, *The Story of Canadian Roads*, (University of Toronto Press, 1966), p. 75.

CHAPTER 8

All the Road's a Stage

THE DUSTY byways were pressed by paws, as well as hooves and wheels in days gone by. Wild animal shows were popular and people travelled many miles to see the exotic presentations. Any change in routine was welcomed and coppers, nickels and dimes were pulled from deep in pockets to pay the ticket price.

Ontario townships passed bylaws regulating "exhibitions of wax figures, wild animals, wire-dancing, circus-riding and other idle acts or feats which common showmen, circus-riders, mountebanks or jugglers performed."[1] In 1855, the entertainers had to pay a sum of not more than £5 to township treasurers before any and every such exhibition.

"BEAR DANCE" was a headline in an 1885 *Almonte Gazette*. The report stated, "The villagers were not a little surprised to see three bears (guided however by three men) enter the village." They were trained to dance and perform various feats. A collection was taken up, and most of the small change in the village must have been given to the bears because a group of visiting evangelists collected no coins at their meeting that same night. The people obviously preferred the bears' performance.

Three or four men struck the town of Smiths Falls several days later. They led their bears into town bright and early in the morning but did not linger long. They trudged on their way very little richer than when they came, as the townsfolk were not interested in their performance at all.

If black bears were a rarity, one can imagine the interest a pair of polar bears generated long years ago. Around the turn of the century, a man travelled the roads with a pair of hapless polar bears chained together. He made a meagre living picking up a few coppers here and there from the folks of the villages and out in the countryside who paid to see the bears.

Horses were terrified of bears of any colour. If they caught sight of one or got a whiff of one, they would snort and try to run away, bouncing buggy or wagon behind them. As a consequence, the handler made the big white bears lie down in a ditch every time a vehicle approached.

In the early 1900s, another interesting pair travelled the roadways. An organ grinder and his small pet monkey stopped at farmgates and treated the families to gay organ tunes and tricks. After the little show, the monkey passed a cap to gather coins. One time, the level of cooperation from the monkey waned. He scampered up onto a porch roof and would not come down, much to the delight of the children and the frustration of the organ grinder.

Concerts of various sorts were advertised by handbills tacked up on bridges, and in mills, stores and blacksmith shops. The townspeople, as well as those who journeyed by horse and buggy from the back parts of the townships, gathered to see these attractions. They were a critical and canny group who did not suffer a poor performance gladly.

In June 1887, a "HIPPOLYMPIAN SHOW" was advertised on handbills. Graceful feats on the flying wire and "equilibrative" performances were promised and they earned rounds of applause. However the rest of the evening's acrobatic specialties did not impress the spectators and they jeered. The news of the day reported that, "There was nothing in it about which we could truthfully make much favorable comment!"

Great numbers of people travelled from far flung farms to attend a wild beast show in Carleton Place, in August 1900. A review of this circus scathingly reported, "It was the rankest ever attended, all over in three-quarters of an hour!" The audience booed the company and made their thoughts known in no uncertain terms that they had not received their money's worth that evening.

A ventriloquist, accused of communing with evil spirits, gave a performance in 1885. His black arts included grinding out operatic music from an organette. His performance was greeted by a slim house and the verdict on his show was that his tricks were clumsily performed and the whole show was below par. He went on his way, stained with travel, ragged, bent and miserably shod, after yet another poor night that yielded him little more than a few coppers for some food.

Not all presentations were below expectations. In the spring of 1885, handbills were posted in prominent places announcing THE NICKEL PLATE CIRCUS. Bold lettering promised wild animals, equestrian stars, umbrella-eared elephants, lions and tigers, male and female Samsons and a "tattooed Fejee Island cannibal!" Newspaper reports after the show indicated that the audience was most impressed, not with the elephants versus Samson, but rather with a side show featuring Mrs. Jesse James who performed some pretty tall rifle shooting. "She knocked ashes from a cigar in Texas Charlie's mouth, smashed a potato on top of his head and performed other equally clever work that showed that at least some of the gentler sex are equals of the "Lords of Creation" in nerve. Altogether it was an excellent show."[2]

Large handbills and newspaper ads announced a show in the Smiths Falls area in

1915 that promised to open with "the grandest street parade ever seen!" This sight of a lifetime was called STETSON'S BIG SPECTACULAR UNCLE TOM'S CABIN. It featured fifty men, women and children with two special female singers billed as Topsies, as well as donkeys and massive dogs. There were "African Mandolin Players, Buck and Wing Dancers, Shouters and a Genuine Cake Walk" all performed in front of a train carload of beautiful scenery depicting COTTON PICKING and HOME IN THE SOUTH. The variation in ticket prices of 25¢, 35¢ and 50¢ must have indicated where you sat and if indeed you sat, or had to stand at the back.

"FEARFUL, FRIGHTFUL, FRENZIED,

The Nickel Plate Show came to Perth in 1885 and was greeted by applauding crowds.

Note the ramp and arced flight of the young lady's performance with her bicycle. The show was given in Perth in 1915.

FLYING FLIGHT — SPANNING DEATH'S ARCH" were the words emblazoned on posters in Perth in June 1915. Mlle. D'Zizzi—a charming Parisian belle, the only woman to ride a bicycle down a steep incline into space and across a fifty-five-foot yawning death trap—was coming to town. A monstrous street parade, advertised as, "Moving miles of wealth and splendour" accompanied by five brass bands, wound through town. Open dens of fierce wild beasts were an added attraction to Mlle. D'Zizzi's spectacular death-defying act.

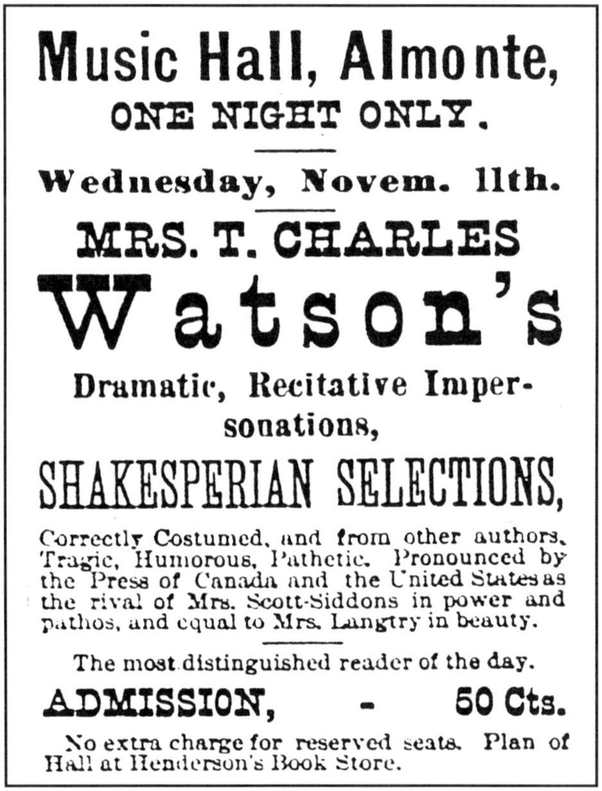

A celebrated elocutionist on tour through the countryside in 1885.

Travelling shows booked halls for their plays, medicine shows, or magic acts and feats of daring. The entertainers often sold souvenirs of glassware and trinkets, as well as medicine such as skunk oil that claimed, among other things, to have wondrous curative powers for arthritic pain. One of these acts was followed by the appearance of a bear from the trunk of an early model car. The well-being of the animals notwithstanding, what fun these travelling medicine shows gave the villagers on summer evenings under the stars. The lantern light glowed and the cries of the showmen and the hoots of the audience echoed into the darkness. Children ran through the crowds, sweethearts clasped hands and elderly folk stood about gossiping and enjoying the show.

The town hall in Middleville was once reserved by a travelling show that featured a gypsy woman who was sawed in half by a cross-cut saw with a long shiny blade. She lay in a rough wooden box, screaming and yelling as the audience watched wide-eyed and captivated. As she was levitated in a later trick to a height of six to eight feet in the air the audience clapped and cheered. Then she was impaled by a pointer while she stood in a hole in the centre of a round table. Childhood recollections of such wonders have stayed vividly in the memory. Medicine was sold after the show. Labeled, "Matthew's Sioux Indian Oil," it sold for fifty cents a bottle and was hailed as a medicine for breathing discomforts and many other maladies. Mixed in this potion of promises were allkuit root, oil of mustard, orgosium, Venice Turps, camphor and wintergreen. Many bottles were purchased and

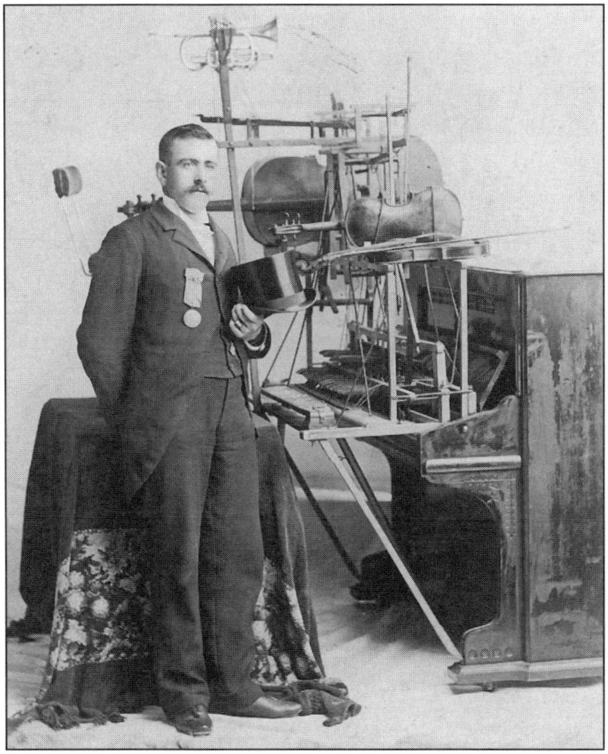

This travelling showman entertained his audiences by playing 23 instruments at the same time. Circa 1890.
COURTESY OF DOROTHY DELAURIER

slipped into pockets to be taken home for an aged parent or an ailing child.

A unique entertainment was held in Perth in 1909. Hailed as a Shredded Wheat Banquet, folks from far and wide were encouraged to come to enjoy an entertainment but also to note the many ways that Shredded Wheat could be used in the production of tempting delicacies. This early product advertising gambit drew large crowds, and agents from Montreal looked after the serving and presentations. People drove home with boxes of Shredded Wheat that were on sale for two packages for twenty-five cents.

Weekly "penny readings" were held in the fall and winter months. People from many communities eagerly hitched up their buggies or sleighs to attend. These public entertainments were an idea brought over from England and began in the 1850s. The idea spread like wildfire as entertainment was rare in both towns and rural districts, except for dances and seasonal festivals. Local performers sang, recited, played music or acted out pantomimes for the intellectual and musical improvement of all. They cost a nickel not a penny, and later a dime. The proceeds of these enthusiastically attended programs were used for worthy causes such as financing a new organ, curtains for a hall or for purchasing books for a newly opened library. They were usually quiet affairs but small boys did tend to get restless.

The skills and talents shared at the penny readings were encouraged by the local singing teachers and music instructors. Due to the enthusiastic interest in music in the communities, there was great call for singing teachers. In the mid- 1800s, a singing master tramped the roads of the county. From his home in Perth, Mr. Doherty walked to Balderson on Monday where he taught the first class. Then on he went to the communities of Prestonvale, Ferguson's Falls and the Tennant-Halpenny settlement, ending up in Clayton on Friday for the last lessons of the week.[3]

At a fee of twenty-five cents per lesson, many families had to scrape together the precious coppers to have their children learn to sing. One talented pupil from Clayton was

Robert Watchorn. When the elderly Mr. Doherty could no longer walk the long distances, Robert took over some of his district. He travelled to teach pupils in Galbraith, Union Hall, Rosetta, Pakenham and Cedar Hill, from November to April when the farm work was less demanding. If Robert was too far from home to return for the night, people gave him food and lodging. His payment in return was to give a family member a free lesson. Penny readings and church choirs in his area benefited greatly from his dedication to his art and pupils.

Some itinerant musical groups offered training as well as entertainment. The Musical Ketchum's Popular Convention Concert Company of Canada presented free concerts in towns and villages. After each concert they hoped to organize a musical convention to encourage the study and development of vocal music in the town. This approach was usually successful and seven-day conventions were duly organized. In 1887 thirty young people joined a class in Lanark. The inspiration to begin local musical associations came from the young people's polished programs of serenades, choruses, glees and anthems that demonstrated their new skills after their study at a Ketchum convention.

Singers, speakers, dramatists and readers of poetry and prose travelled the roads of Ontario. The citizens of Perth and district were treated to an evening's entertainment by a celebrated artist-entertainer who garnered round after round of applause with his rapid crayon work, wonderful powers of mimicry and talent as a singer. Almonte hosted Mrs. T. Charles Watson's Music Hall night in 1885. She offered a selection of dramatic, recitative impersonations and Shakespearean selections. Advertised as, "The most distinguished reader of the day," she used correct costuming and the price of admission was a mere fifty cents. The crowds were well behaved and enthusiastic about her skills. Not all presentations were attended by such attentive audiences. Often the performers had to be on their toes to deal with the catcalls of drunken hecklers and contend with brawls.

Some performances were low-key, highly individual and much appreciated. One such fellow did not need to worry about jeers and cat calls, but perhaps only a slightly raised eyebrow or a quiet scoff as he shared tales of his adventures and the local news with families by the evening firelight. This familiar visitor was an entertaining Scot known as Old Patterson. This genial fellow and his constant canine companion Gippy, periodically trudged the Perth Road from end to end. Every few months, at farms along his accustomed route, someone in the family would inquire, "Is it not aboot time Old Patterson and Gippy wes pullin' at the latch string?" Without fail, his figure was soon seen coming up the laneway.

A visit from Patterson was an occasion for him to bring the families up to date on the news and gossip of the farms along the road. He performed the role of travelling newspaper through the back townships when newspapers with local news were scarce. In the main, the tid-bits of gossip the old man repeated were sufficiently accurate as to detail, but among the older folks some of his tales were received with due reservation.

However, with the art of a consummate storyteller, the Scot was an inspiration to the boys and girls of the homesteads. As he told them some of his experiences and of the things he had seen, he emphasized the important parts by tapping the floor with his gnarled thorn stick. Patterson was the first person to invest their existence with a kind of glamour. Listening to his tales, ". . . life took on a golden sheen and all clouds had silver linings."[4]

Old Patterson's travels took him as far from Lanark County as the Glengary area. His faithful Gippy is buried there in a specially marked grave that tells of his travels and of the service the two gave to the settlers of the back country.

Popular performances were put on in local inns and taverns when the boisterous shantymen were in town. Legendary men like Chain Lightning Stewart and the very spry Larry Frost regaled the nightime crowds with tales of the bush, their white water escapades and monster loads of timber. Plaster was removed from more than one ceiling where Larry Frost left the impression of both his boot heels from a single spring from the floor or where he cartwheeled with sinewy power to leave his boot caulk marks in the ceiling beams.

Visitors of a different stripe ventured into the towns, villages and hamlets of the county in the late 1800s. Evangelical groups selling doctrine, not peddling lace and ribbons, travelled from town to town, holding revival meetings and religious entertainments. Skeptically compared to salesman by some people, they were called "pedlars of divinity."

> A camp meeting was held in Smiths Falls in August, 1889. "Every available horse, wagon and boat in town was in demand. Two thousand people attended."
>
> The *Rideau Record*

On a warm June evening in 1887, the famous White Brothers gave one of their sacred concerts in the Lanark townhall. The hall was filled with an appreciative and orderly audience, including people from considerable distance. They enjoyed gospel songs, humorous moral songs and songs of a practical bearing. It was a rare musical treat and was praised by the pious country folk for the good that must follow such singing and earnest exhortation.

One of the White Brothers must have made an enemy some evening along the way—whether over religious inclinations, ticket prices or some ugly exchange with a rowdy heckler from the audience. In 1899, the singing evangelist's farm buildings in western Ontario were set on fire and piles of sawn lumber from his mill also went up in smoke. One step further was taken by the unknown, vengeful blackguard. He drove nails into the mill's unsawn logs which went through the saw at great expense in broken teeth and also with considerable danger to the sawyers. A reward of five hundred dollars was offered to anyone helping to apprehend Mr. White's persecutor.

Visiting evangelist preachers, Messr's Crossley and Hunter, held revival meetings in Lanark in 1909, and the content of their sermons were inspiring and profitable. People welcomed these "hot shots" to awaken their consciences to principles and practices. No hall was big enough to hold all the people attracted to the meetings. A free will offering was taken up for the preachers but success was measured in the signing up of four hundred and ninety-six souls affirming or renewing their allegiance to the Lord.[5] Hornerite or Holiness Movement evangelists from distant cities visited communities where there were congregations of followers. The Hornerites of Boyd Settlement welcomed a Mr. Coleman in 1899 and the revival meetings were well attended. Reports said that much good was being done.

People gathered in towns and villages for the revival meetings, concerts and circuses but parades brought out the biggest crowds. Noisy, colourful parades were an essential part of any celebration in years past. Bands, trades floats, costumed marchers, many horse drawn vehicles and new fire fighting equipment were all part of the parades at fairs and special occasions. St. Patrick's Day was often celebrated with a parade, as was the great national holiday, May 24th—the Queen's birthday.

TO THE DRIVING PUBLIC

THE UNDERSIGNED is prepared to supply the public with good reliable outfits–both single and double. Buggies are comfortable and stylish and horses are all good roadsters. All calls, either at stable or by telephone, will be promptly attended to.

Having purchased a power Clipper I am prepared to do horse clipping at any time.
Prices reasonable.

A. W. BAIRD

Lanark, March 20th, '98

A livery stable advertisement from the *Lanark Era* in 1898.

In 1896, the May celebrations almost caused a duel between two young chaps over a buggy. James Bowes, a livery stable owner in Lanark, had introduced the first top-buggy in the district. He promised the first drive to his most valued customer, a young lad hoping to impress his sweetheart. They were to drive to the 24th of May celebrations in Perth in the

An oak tree was planted by George Pretty to mark the royal visit of The Prince of Wales in 1860. Mr. Pretty stands beside the tree in 1939 with his wife Janet and her brother Abe. COURTESY OF LILLIAN SWEENEY

new vehicle. An obstacle appeared when it was found that his rival had removed one of the wheels of the new buggy. The young couple, not to be deterred from taking their pleasure, secured the next best carriage. Upon returning from Perth, tempers flared between the two rival swains and the incident might have been the cause for a fatal duel had friends not intervened.

A popular feature of the Queen's birthday celebration parades, held in the county seat of Perth, was military displays with local militiamen in various uniforms. These continued from the early days of settlement when Provincial Militia Acts demanded manpower for defense. The Acts were in effect until the 1850s. Under these regulations men from the ages of sixteen to sixty were obliged to serve in the militia. They mustered for one training day each year, marching and drilling in large fields wherever the captain of their area ordered. Training Day was held on the 4th of June, the birthday of King George III.

In June 1837, two hundred men appeared from the wilds of their farms to drill in a field, at the farm of James Fair in Dalhousie Township. Few were in uniform but all were earnest defenders of the flag. This large turnout was due to the reports of political unrest in Lower Canada and the rumblings of rebellion in Upper Canada as well. On December 6, 1837, George Easton noted in his diary, "The left wing of the 1st Regiment of the Lanark Militia paraded and got a volunteer offer to go to Lower Canada and five men went." Then in January 1838, "Our Militiamen marched from Dalhousie on the 12th of January." It was with relief that he noted on February 17, 1838, "Some of our volunteers came home from the war."

Patriotism and loyalty to the sovereign Queen Victoria ran high in the blood of the immigrants from Great Britain. In 1860, Albert Edward, Prince of Wales, visited Ottawa and the Ottawa Valley. He travelled from Arnprior to Almonte by carriage and he was cheered and greeted with great hospitality all along the route. In the spirit of history and respect due the Prince's visit, a commemorative oak sapling was planted in Darling Township by seventeen-year-old George G. Pretty. It flourished and seventy-nine years later Mr. Pretty hung a picture of Queen Victoria on the lofty tree and posed for a picture beside his piece of living history.

Patriotism for another cause was manifested in the Orange parades on "the Glorious Twelfth" of July. Held alternately in Carleton Place, Perth and Smiths Falls, they were always well attended. A man was chosen to represent the host Orange Lodge and as King Billy, he rode a big, grey horse at the head of the parade. The horse was garlanded with pompoms, paper flowers and wore a big hoop, festooned with flowers over its head. King Billy rode at the head of the procession through the main streets of town. July 12th marked an ancient victory. The parades celebrated past memories of Ireland and King William at the Battle of the Boyne in 1690. They fostered ongoing prejudice between Protestants and Catholics for years, long after many people thought the parades should be discontinued.

In commemoration of the first anniversary of Confederation in 1868, a parade was held in the village of Middleville called "The Terrible's Celebration."[6] The parade was made up of rowdy, colourfully costumed marchers ringing cowbells and blowing horns. "Terribles'" also marched in Lanark led by a mounted captain and martial music. Community picnics and games were part of these celebrations. Village picnics always included the highjinks of young people and these often included wriggling garter snakes that set youngsters screaming. One young woman wearing a wide full skirt in the fashion of the day, was lifted up and set down over a tall, old burdock plant which was resplendent with a good crop of loose burrs. Hilarity and sympathy were the conflicting sentiments about this prank which probably broke down along gender lines.

Middleville rolled out the red carpet for one of its own in January, 1900. Miss Minnie Affleck, a trained nurse, was one of the nurses who accompanied the First Contingent to South Africa for duty in the Boer War. When she returned from her stint in the army, she was met in Perth by a reception committee with a carriage and pair all gaily decorated. As the procession, accompanied by the band of the 42nd Regiment, passed through Lanark on its nineteen-mile journey to Middleville, large numbers of citizens turned out to cheer her return. Passing out of Lanark under evergreen arches, the band struck up once again and the procession resumed its march. A torchlight procession was organized in Middleville before the townsfolk packed the

A parade along Gore Street in Perth. Circa 1900. The town's steam fire engine was a feature of the parade. PA-79241

town hall for an official reception in the evening.

With the outbreak of the First World War, long files of young men in uniform marched down the streets of Smiths Falls and Perth on their way to the train stations to board the cars

SOLDIERS' RECEPTION and CELEBRATION

The Citizens of Carleton Place will tender a Public Reception to the Returned Soldiers of the Town on

Saturday, August 16th

the event taking the form of a Day of Sports and Entertainment, followed by a Supper and presentation to the returned men in the Town Hall.

The programme will open with

A Monster PROCESSION

in the morning, in the afternoon a Programme of Sports at Riverside Park, concluding with a Band Concert and Fireworks in the evening. The Sports include

A Baseball MATCH

Between the Senecas of Ottawa and Perth

LACROSSE Match

Carleton Place vs. Almonte

Foot Races, Tugs-of-War, &c., &c.

The G.W.V.A. Band of Ottawa

will furnish music during the day and evening.

General Admission, 25 cts; Children, 15 cts

Soldiers and their families free.

FIREWORKS AND BAND CONCERT

in the evening in the Town Park. - Admission free.

Invitations have been issued to all returned Soldiers. Any failing to receive one will kindly report to the Mayor without delay.

Citizens are asked to decorate and assist in making the day a success

A celebration for returned soldiers was announced in the *Carleton Place Herald* in 1919.

GRAND ASSEMBLY

WILL BE HELD IN

McDONALD'S CORNERS HALL

Friday, March 1st, 1918

Good Music, Good Time, Refreshments,

Come and Bring Your Friends

Tickets, $1 a Couple   Extra Ladies Free

GRAND ASSEMBLY

The Young Men of the Village will hold an Assembly,

IN

Town Hall,

MIDDLEVILLE

ON

Thursday. March 8th, '18

Tickets Including Supper, $1 a Couple

Ladies Free

PROCEEDS DONATED TO RED CROSS.

Assemblies or dances were held to raise money for worthy causes. In 1918 proceeds were being donated to the Red Cross. *LANARK ERA*, MARCH, 1918 that would bear them away from their native land to fight on foreign soil. The route was lined with friends and loved ones waving and choking back tears and fears.

Local groups left on the home front organized events to bolster spirits in the difficult days of the war. A "Grand Triumphal Pageant Procession" was held in McDonald's Corners in 1915. The village was long famous for its parades and pageants but this one topped them all. Represented in the parade was every country at war in Europe. Even the Kaiser of Germany was to appear in the pageant, accompanied by music bands, clowns and cowboys. This parade heralded a large baseball tournament with a shanty dinner at noon and an evening supper. People flocked to the village from every quarter and horses were tied to any available fence rail or stabled wherever there was a space.

At the end of the war in 1918, the soldiers who survived the raging carnage that was the First World War, returned home to their families. The war heroes were fêted and treated royally at banquets with speeches in their honour and gifts of commemorative rings or watches. Joyous parades along specially decorated routes welcomed the soldiers home. People waved flags and bands played to rejoice in the war's end.

Dances were held in villages and towns everywhere to raise funds for the Red Cross to provide aid to the soldiers as well as for families in need in war ravaged countries. The dances were called assemblies, which was an old term brought from Scotland. Whirling, winding country dances and square dances brought roses to the cheeks of the young people who danced until dawn and then had to get home to the serious business of working on a farm.

---

1 *The Municipal Manual for Upper Canada*, Fifth Edition, 1885, p. 23.
2 The *Almonte Gazette*, July 3, 1885.
3 Jane Watchorn Wright, *A Voice To Sing His Praises*, From a scrapbook Courtesy of the Middleville and District Museum.
4 Dee Mac Enne, (Donald McNicol), From a scrapbook, Courtesy of the Watson's Corners Museum.
5 The *Lanark Era*, May 19, 1909.
6 Jean Rankin, Scrapbook, Courtesy of the Middleville and District Museum.

CHAPTER 9

Were There Ever Such People?

GYPSY people emigrated from Europe in the last quarter of the 19th century and often travelled into Canada from the United States. Were there ever such people on the roads of Lanark County? Yes! According to numerous and colourful reports, these travelling folk were seen on the dusty highways and byways from the late 1800s until the 1930s.

Evidence of the gypsies' passing was found in the grass near a blackened circle of stones by the roadside near Hopetown. It was a tiny silver revolver that must have fallen from the pocket of a gypsy woman's skirt when her family made camp near the creek. Other traces of gypsies were found at many places around the county. The camp sites they chose were often under the sheltering boughs of a tall elm at a crossroads, near a long handled pump in an empty summer schoolyard or beside a flowing stream where fresh water for cooking, washing and watering their horses was close at hand. Their campfire circles were littered with eggshells, the chips of green wood cut for their cooking fires, horse droppings and even the occasional horseshoe.

The gypsies' arrival near a town or farming settlement didn't mean trouble, but it did mean anxiety. At the sight of a passing gypsy caravan, front porch rocking chairs abruptly stilled as folks held their breath and tensely waited for the strangers to pass by. People were dubious of these foreign looking folk and tales of treachery, though not of violence, preceded them. Signs barring them from certain buildings and areas of towns were not uncommon.

Gypsy families usually travelled alone, although occasionally the parents and a grown son and his family would travel in a small procession. Two-seat, double buggies were used, as well as a flat wagon to carry their tents, blankets, utensils and all the paraphernalia needed for their itinerant life-style. Some gypsy families travelled in the hoop-topped caravans so typical in gypsy lore.

The caravans or "vardos," as they were called in the Romany language, had a canvas flap cover that rolled down at the back to keep out the dust of the roadways and to prevent the eyes of strangers from prying into the depths of their travelling homes. A water pail hung on the back axle, and several spare horses were tied to rings on the sides to lead them along the miles until they were traded. Foals often trotted along beside their mothers who pulled the wagons.

Followed by lean, lanky dogs and several bare-footed, berry-brown children, the caravans travelled from place to place. The families would find a "halt" for a night or for several days, nestled in a secluded meadow beside a brook or in a pine-needled dell in a dry hollow for protection from summer storms.

When the family drew rein on their team for the night, the creak of the bow-topped wagon and the rumble of wheels ceased for awhile. Out came a small tent or two and the horses were unharnessed. A big black cooking pot was slung on a rod held over a campfire by two stakes in the ground. Soon the campsite was filled with the smell of woodsmoke and the hissing sound of burning green wood. Steam from the bubbling pot flew off on the breeze as the gypsies settled in for the night.

The men with long handle bar mustaches lounged around smoking their pipes while the women worked away, cooking and washing, often with youngsters on their hips. Wet clothing was hung on any convenient branches or fence near the campsite or on a rope looped from the caravan to a nearby tree.

The gypsy horses were hobbled with hames straps around their front feet and let loose for the night to graze on what they could find by the road or in waste meadows. These horses were healthy and hardy. Gypsies believed that animals allowed to forage freely, selected the plants that they needed for good health. Their horses grazed on the roadsides and all the herbs and vitamin-rich weeds they needed were available.

Wild plants were used by the gypsies to treat ailments in horses: burdock and nettles for hair growth, brambles for skin lesions, cowslip

Marie, a young gypsy woman camped along the roadside in 1909. PA- C21159

and hops to quiet nervous or excitable animals, plantain for eye disorders and ragwort for drawing impurities from tumours and fistulas. The healing properties of elder, tansy and hazel were especially prized by gypsies. Brow bands of woven hazel twigs were sometimes attached to horses' bridles to protect them from ill luck.[1]

Wild vegetable plants and potherbs that had succulent, tuberous roots, or nutritious leaves and stems, were all part of the gypsy diet. Medicinal herbs from fields and woods were gathered as well. Tales are told of farm children being cured by elderly, gypsy women with knowledge of natural remedies.

The gypsies gleaned what wild food they could from the roadways too. The sweetness of wild berries, plums, cherries, rosehips and apples, as well as the bitterness of haws, cranberries, nuts, and mushrooms were sampled as the seasons turned. Complaints were made that, "Gypsies picked the berries before you could ever get to them." But roadside berries and fruits were free for the taking and gypsies lived so close to nature that they knew exactly when each fruit ripened.

Gypsy girls on the way to a spring near their camp in 1926. PA-87487

The gypsies made their way by trading horses, tinkering and telling fortunes. Being proud and clannish people, they had little use for the "gadge" or non-gypsy. As they travelled the countryside, they ignored and were ignored by most people. Farmers and commercial travellers seldom exchanged waves or friendly greetings with the gypsies as they passed on the roadways.

It is said that the gypsies spoke with a twang in their broken English but they could get by well enough to carry out their deals. The men were slick horse traders. Usually trading in light horses, you would find them ready to sell or trade at any time. Farming folk needed heavy horses for field work, so not much trading was carried on in the countryside. Nearer the towns, dealing was brisk as people wanted lighter, faster horses for pulling buggies and sleighs.

People often saved unruly horses that balked, bit or kicked to trade to the gypsies. Horses led to a gypsy camp were sometimes part of a deal that traded bad horses for worse. Gypsy horses, sound and free moving at the time of the trade, would churn with the heaves or develop a severe limp after the gypsies left town and the effects of their medicinal herbs such as tansy and comfry wore off.

Gypsies were noted for having a way with horses. They had centuries of horse lore and experience behind them. As often as not, a bad horse was straightened out with gypsy handling and then sold to someone who was pleased with his purchase. Such a story was told by Annie Barr of Ramsay township about a young farm girl who had lots of chores to do. She asked her father for a horse and he said, "Whenever the gypsies come 'round, we'll go down." In due time, the gypsies camped near their village and a deal was struck for a jet black horse. The young girl rode that horse to school and it saved her miles of walking to fetch in the cows. She also harnessed it to a buggy to drive to town to get supplies. When asked if the horse kicked and bit, she replied, "No. It was the nicest horse ever brought onto our property!" It was a valued part of the farm for many years. So not all gypsy deals were sour ones.

The gypsy women were as cunning as the men in their wheedling and dealing. A wiry, old gypsy women entered the Rosedale Cheese Factory at Union Hall one morning. She saw a cheese in the curing room and asked, "How much for the big cheese?" The cheesemaker said, "If you can carry it, you can have it." She promptly heaved it onto her shoulder and made for the door. It was a ninety-pound cheese! The amazed cheesemaker had to stop her and more courteously tell her the price of the cheese.

The darkly tanned gypsy women wore long trailing skirts. "They walked like as if they were waltzing" were the words used to describe the swaying of the colourful long skirts of the gypsy women of childhood memory. A bright scarf, knotted at the nape of the neck covered their straight black hair for sun protection as well as a touch of modesty. Red, blue and green were favoured colours for sashes, scarves and skirts.

"They were great ones for jewelery" is an often imparted bit of information. "Fairly hanging with beads" is another description of a gypsy and her jewelry. Big earrings and bracelets jingled as the women went about their work and heavy necklaces of coins flashed in the sunlight.

Lovely lace fancy work, bead work and wicker or rush baskets were turned out by quick, nimble fingers, perhaps as the women rode in the caravans putting to good use the hours of jolting and bumping along over the stony and rutted roads.

From camps near communities, the gypsy women walked into town with large baskets of wares. Going from door to door they sold their handiwork or made a trade for some garden produce, meat or used children's clothing. In 1896, a band of gypsies visited Lanark Village for an afternoon. While the women peddled tinware door to door, the men stood off by themselves content to watch their horses graze.[2]

That gypsies "had a name for stealing children" was a common belief, and this struck fear into the hearts of youngsters. The cry of "Here come the gypsies!" was always enough to send children on the run for school, into the woods to hide, or straight for home. Dashing past a gypsy camp on the way to or from school was an ordeal of terror, but also of fascination for the children, as their bright eyes took in every detail of the setting.

A story that might explain why the child-stealing stories persisted, tells of a small girl who disappeared about the same time as the gypsies passed through the Fitzroy area. Sorrow was heavy at her family farm but it intensified for the farmer when he found the child's small shoes in the pig pen. He never told his wife of the tragedy and let her believe their daughter was alive and well with the gypsies.

This threat of gypsies was a frightening thing in the old days but the recollections of Charles Pretty were different. He remembered a kindly, old gypsy lady camped beside a stream near Hopetown. She gave him a dish of delicious beans ladled out of a big iron pot that had been buried all night under hot coals in the sand. He received "an awful tonguing" from his father when he got home. He was warned that he could have been stolen. However, Charlie did not believe the gypsies wanted to take him along on their travels and the memory of those sand-baked beans lasted over the decades. Another "sweet" gypsy reminiscence involved the huge crocks of jam that gypsies kept in the back of their wagons. They were sticky pots of fascination for farm children whenever they approached a gypsy camp because occasionally, they were allowed to poke a finger into the jam.

> "The band of gypsies that have been tenting in Middleville have taken their departure."
> *Lanark Era,* April, 1898.

One day, in the summer of 1916, a gypsy caravan stopped in front of one of the general stores in Middleville. On the way into the store a lovely-looking young gypsy woman was able to wheedle a dollar from a man sitting on the steps. The gypsies looked around the store and bought a few things. It was the habit of businessmen, in those days, to carry a large roll of bills in their pocket and seeing the storekeeper's money, the young woman blew a breath of good luck into it. Then they went on their way.

In a few moments the storekeeper was running up to the local mill wanting to hire one of the only two cars in the village at the time to chase the gypsies. He said they had made off with some of his money. A quick telephone call down the road verified that the gypsies were heading for Brightside so the storekeeper drove quickly to Lanark to get the constable. Joined by several soldiers who were on leave from the 130th Lanark and Renfrew Regiment, they all set out to find the caravan. The "boys in khaki" were ordered to leave their guns behind but they refused and the constable was reminded that soldiers in training were never issued any ammunition.

At Craig's store in Brightside the pursuing party was told that the gypsies had turned up the Lammermoor road. Over the way they found the caravan at the side of the road with the horses tied to the wagons eating hay while the gypsy families were sitting around a fire drinking from tin mugs.

The constable approached them and ordered them to return the money but their only answer was to shake their heads and say a few words in a foreign language. The young woman would not speak and they all pretended not to understand English. The soldiers decided to take things into their own hands. They stepped out of their car with their guns at the ready.

Then the scene changed. The gypsies leaped to their feet and held up their hands and cried, "Don't shoot. Don't shoot. We'll give you the money you want." Their leader went among them and collected a few dollars from each until they had the right amount of money. They did not admit their guilt and acted as if a ransom was being collected from them.[3] There is no way of ascertaining if indeed the travellers had whisked away some of the storekeeper's money or not.

People believed that gypsies stole things at night. The axe was always brought in from the chopping block and no wash was left on the clothes-line overnight. Favourite dogs were called in early in the evening, as it was thought they would fall prey to the travelling folk and disappear. In 1897, a band of gypsies came into White Lake and local reports said that they did not apear to be of the most honourable character. The storekeepers of the town "did quite a business in padlocks" and it was the wish of the community that the gypsies' stay be short.

The talk of stealing was not all exaggeration. Adeline James used to occasionally hear the rattle of milk cans left in the creek. The evening milk was kept cool in the water all night but was easy prey for gypsies. Another family found a hair comb in a can of milk that had been left to keep cool in the spring overnight. When milk was poured off for the family breakfast one morning, the hair comb washed out into the pitcher. No explanation could be given except that a gypsy woman must have taken some milk during the night and lost her comb in the process.

Gypsy people often asked for fresh water or came up a lane way calling, "Halloo. Halloo. Got a sick woman." Sometimes they wanted a

A gypsy camp scene in October, 1918. PA-71167

chicken or some eggs. Often they begged for milk for a newborn baby. Whether or not there was a baby, people were never sure.

Sometimes grain was demanded for the horses. This was a frightening predicament for a farm woman if she was home alone with small children. With her men folk out in the fields, and gypsies at the door, she felt obliged to give the hand-out but feared as well, that when she went to get the feed, one of them might go into the house and steal something.

The Wilson family of Fitzroy Harbour remembered a suppertime visit of a small group of gypsies years and years ago. They came in uninvited and spoke to each person in turn. "Hello Grandpa." "Hello Grandma." They coaxed for food but were refused ham and chicken off the table. A middle-aged gypsy woman stayed near the grandfather, petting him and pitying him. "Oh, you are so old. You will die soon. Oh, you are so old." Finally, when they had gone, it was discovered that so was the grandfather's money! Fifteen dollars in total. A single nickel was left in his pocket. When their outrage cooled, it was an oft-repeated family joke that this was all the gypsy woman had thought he would probably need for the rest of his short life.

In the fall of the year, the night dews became heavier and the cricket songs slowed to a dull hum around the gypsy campsites. Tents were left folded and the gypsies slept in their caravans up off the cold, damp ground. Gypsies visited the poultry fairs held in many communities in November. They bought frozen chickens and pork before they headed south to

A gypsy camp near Peterborough, Ontario in 1909. Being continually on the move, the gypsy groups appeared sporadically in many parts of Ontario. PA- C21153

the United States. Then they had to set a fast pace to reach the warmer climes before the snows flew. No wheels rolled in the winter.

Not all the gypsy families were able to get south in time as illustrated by news in the *Almonte Gazette* of February, 1888. A family of gypsies had been hanging about in a deserted house near the agricultural hall for a few weeks. They had an exciting time getting their horse up out of the cellar. The animal was stabled in the kitchen and fell through the floor.

The gypsies became less conspicuous on the roadways as horsepower gave way to the motor car. They travelled around the countryside in cars and in the 1930s they were most often seen outside the grounds of country show-fairs. The gypsy men were not welcome inside the fairgrounds because they were suspected of pick-pocketing in the crowds. The women were eyed cautiously as they sat in front of small tents, brightly clothed and tinkling with jewelry, cajoling the fair-goers into having their fortunes told. Interested people ducked into the gypsy tent to have a palm read or to see the future unfold in an ordinary deck of cards or in the more exotic pictures of a tarot deck.

Gone now are the black circles of ash from gypsy campfires. Gone are the evenings when people, returning home from a meeting, a dance or a social, saw the flickering of their campfires or heard the music from a gypsy concertina or violin floating on the breeze, blending with the call of a whippoorwill or the hoot of an owl.

Rosie, a fourteen-year-old gypsy bride at a camp near Peterborough, Ontario in 1909. PA- C21154

---

[1] Juliette de Bairacli Levy, *Herbal Handbook for Farm and Stable*, (Rodale Press Inc. 1976).
[2] The *Lanark Era*, October 28, 1896.
[3] Mrs. Mary Morrison, Scrapbook.

Personal Interviews From 1986-1994:

Annie Barr, William Bolger, Lillian Corkery, Norman Dunlop, William Drynan, Everett Findlay, Mr. & Mrs. M. Foster, Alice McIntosh, Mr. & Mrs. David McIntosh, Allie McKay, Len McKay, May Oates, Charles Pretty, Lillian Sweeney, and Helen Wilson.

CHAPTER 10

From Horseshoes to Hubcaps

AS THE LAST years of the 1800s rolled into the new century, bicycles became popular. "Wheels" as they were called, were awkward to ride on the rough roads where wagon wheels and horses' hooves left ruts and ridges. Careless driving also caused problems when people were learning how to handle their new machines. Newspapers reported local bicycling news in the early 1900s.

> On Saturday evening last, two cyclists collided with each other in front of the Clyde Hotel in Lanark and as a result, one of them had a pedal off his wheel. "Cease scorching around corners boys!" was the advice given by the editor.

> An Almonte man with at least "three sheets in the wind" tried to run over a little girl on a bicycle last week. Result: a bruised girl, a broken wheel and a bill of damage for the teamster.

Automobiles began to make their appearance in the early years of the 20th century so bicycles were not the only newfangled contraptions on the roadways. The sight and sound of these noisy, motorized vehicles was hard on horses. They snorted and rolled their eyes when they had to face oncoming cars. Teams were quickly turned into any nearby yard to take refuge as soon as the sound of an automobile was in the air. Farm families became used to neighbours' teams and travellers' rigs alike turning into their lanes to avoid meeting cars.

Considerate automobile drivers slowed down or stopped to let uneasy horses pass. Many horses were calm about cars once they got used to them but some never accepted having to share the road and stood on their hind legs or bolted at the merest whiff of gasoline. Passengers always jumped safely out of the wagon or buggy before skittish horses were led past an automobile along the road. Some municipalities made an effort to control the effect automobiles had on horses. One

Wheels for ladies and gentlemen cost forty dollars or so in the early 1900s as advertised in the *Lanark Era*.

Tailors began specializing in "Bicycle Toggery" for enthusiasts. LANARK ERA, 1900

bylaw "required the driver of a car to put a canvas painted with country scenery over his car if a horsedrawn vehicle refused to go by."[1]

Traction engines had shared the road with horses for years before the automobile, but not on a daily basis. Strict bylaws concerning these very large engines were in place if safety concerns arose. The engine driver was expected to stop the machine and assist the person to pass the engine with his horse or team if there was even the prospect of difficulty. Teamsters had managed to accommodate the presence of these big engines on the road as their presence was seasonal. However, with the swift rise in the numbers of cars on the road, they had to share their previously undisputed possession of the roadways every time they headed their teams to town.

> Articles in farm and town journals of the time advised that allowances had to be made for horses. "Give the horseman a chance—the car is easier managed"
>
> The *Canadian Countryman*, 1917

In the early days of automobiles, there was a stand-off between teamsters and automobile enthusiasts. The roads had been made by the labour of horses, for horses and horsepower was praised by the populace as shown in this folk song snippet.

Old Dobbin was here, Old Dobbin was there,
First off to the market, then off to the fair.
He would run to the hay-field and tug up the
 hill
With ale for the reapers or corn for the mill.[2]

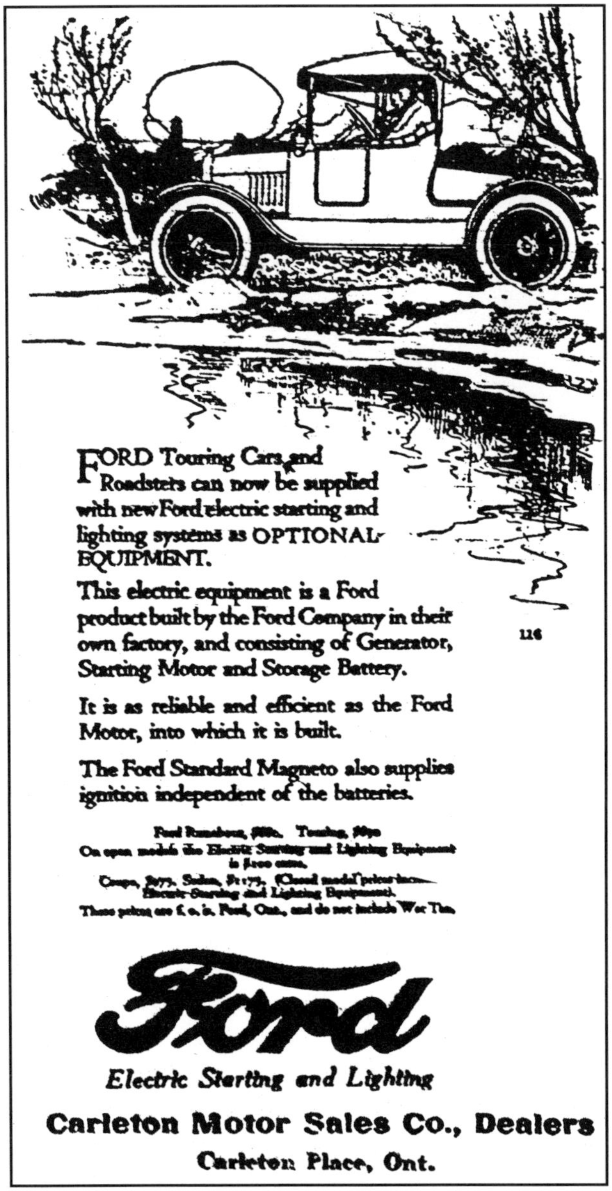

Ford Touring cars were advertised in 1919 in the *Carleton Place Herald*. Their virtues included getting to town quickly for supplies as well as wooing a sweetheart.

Arguments were in the air at auction sales, church festivals, cheese factory picnics, shooting matches and threshings. Wherever people gathered, the debate raged about the merits of live versus mechanized horsepower.

> "No matter how bad the flies may be, my truck will not stamp its feet, switch its tail or kick over the traces. It will not shy even when it meets a lunatic hurrying to the grave astride a motorcycle."
>
> "Horses cost less to buy."
>
> "My truck will not lie down and roll in a cow lot and then look injured because it has not been curried. It does not blow its nose in my face and use my Sunday shirt as a handkerchief just as we leave for church."
>
> "Horses don't depreciate as fast."
>
> "My truck isn't going to get tangled up in a wire fence the night before I want to take my grain to market."
>
> "My horse always welcomes me in the morning."
>
> "Cup grease is cheaper than gall cure and it takes me farther."

Elaborate calculations were done by the car industry to show how inefficient horses were. They promoted their new product by calling horses profit eaters. It was proposed that man works for horse more than horse works for man when you consider the harness makers, tanners, whip makers, stable workers, veterinarians, street cleaners, planters and harvesters of horse feed and the men who make the machinery with which to do it. Statistics said the average farm horse worked actually 3.5 hours a day. He eats 10 pounds of feed for every hour or 12,000 pounds per year which is the production of five acres of ground.[3] The push was on to nudge faithful old Dobbin into retirement and move into the power age of the gasoline engine.

People resisting the modern transportation changes confidently pronounced that a drive with a fast stepping team was more exhilarating than the consumption of an automobile cocktail composed of fifty parts road dust and an equal quantity of nauseating gasoline odours. Assertions were made that horses would always start on a cold morning and indeed when snow drifts blocked the country roads, often the rural mail drivers had to engage teams to replace their automobiles to get the mail through.

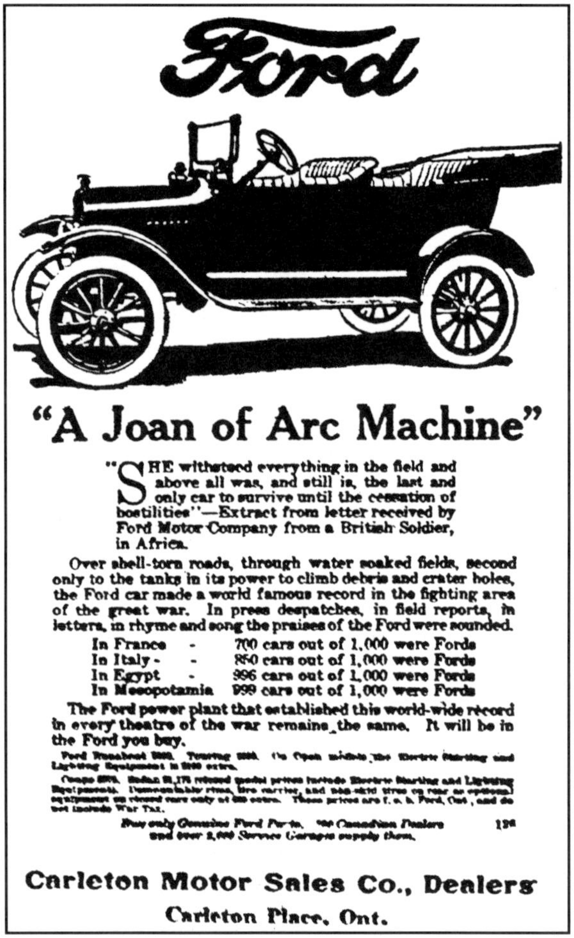

A car advertisement in the *Carleton Place Herald* of 1919 lauding the Ford car for its durability in the shell-torn roads of Europe. Perhaps a comparison was being made with the country roads of Ontario.

The hooting of a car horn was a complete puzzle to people of towns and villages the first time a horseless carriage arrived on their streets. Usually the approach was signaled by the blowing horn and everybody inside hotels and stores rushed out to see what the ungodly racket was. They marveled at the new machine that marked a new era in transportation.

In 1907, the Herron family from Herron's Mills had an "automobile party." The news spread quickly as people exclaimed to friends and relatives in other parts of the county, "What do you think? We had an automobile in our village yesterday. It kept travelling back and forth between Middleville and Herron's Mills. The automobile belonged to the Gillies. It chased Bob Reid's white horse all the way up the road to Middleville. The horse was nearly scared out of its wits. Mrs. Robert Affleck thought that Bob was going to be run over. She was out in the middle of the road yelling for them to stop but Bob was away down the road and around a corner. Her efforts were to no avail." Amidst the excitement it was agreed by all that the new vehicle was "a dandy."

Farming families often took their ease on the front porch in the evening after the day's work was done. In district after district, gasps of apprehension were drawn in the night air as strange, bright lights were seen coming down the concession lines. The vehicles sporting the lights puttered on past, but not before a pulse of alarm disturbed the calm of the long to be remembered night the first automobile went by.

> Local news in 1922 had this warning, "It is watch the crossings now, for two new cars have arrived in Tatlock. Mr. Thomas King and Mr. Robert G. Barr are the purchasers."

Popular wisdom forecast that motorized vehicles would displace horses as surely as horses had displaced the ox. Cars were hailed as a greater convenience to the average farm family than the telephone, the rural mail or even the grain binder. Traffic patterns were changing and farming families were no longer pioneers isolated on their land. Farmers were businessmen and the slow beat of their horses' hooves was the beat of times past. There were now choices to be made, choices that speeded life up.

Automobile advertising banner headlines read:

MODERN CONDITIONS DEMAND MODERN APPLIANCES

MORE SPEED, LESS SWEAT

ON THE JOB WHEN YOU NEED THEM– COST NO FEED WHEN YOU DON'T

IF YOU HAVE NEVER DRIVEN A FORD YOU HAVE SOMETHING TO LEARN ABOUT MOTORING.[4]

By 1917, teamsters had just about abandoned the idea that they should have an exclusive right to the roads. Automobile drivers and horsemen came to terms with sharing the road and a protocol for travelling the roads was accepted. Those handling the ribbons had to have the courtesy to let a faster vehicle pass and give it room to do so. However, a car driver's most provoking situation was the case where a teamster appeared not to hear the horn or hearing it, out of cussedness or selfishness, refused to turn aside to let the car pass.

This Ford truck advertisement says it all about the convenience on offer to the farmers. *THE POWER AGE*, 1920

Ford automobiles were the popular car everywhere. The cost of running a Ford was claimed to be less than half the expense of other cars. A car dealer who handled Fords for Perth, Lanark and Smiths Falls received train car loads of them. In 1915, the new models came equipped with electric lights, a speedometer, a cowl dash, a ventilating windshield and boasted a beautiful painted finish.

Model T Fords had a fuel pump near the front of the gas tank. When driving up a hill all the gas ran to the back and none went to the engine. On steep hills often the car stalled and had to be backed down the hill, turned around and backed up the hill to keep the gas going to the pump. This was but a small price to pay for the modern convenience of automobile travel.

> An early taxi service between Lanark village and Perth was advertised in 1915. A scheduled automobile service set out twice daily for a fare of only one dollar. The car stopped along the way at private residences when requested.
>
> *Lanark Era*, June, 1919.

In front of far flung country stores, gas pumps sprang up like a new kind of vegetation and steam vulcanizers, that were used to repair tires that hissed with punctures, were a new feature at blacksmith shops. Gasoline charges were prohibitive for some families. A humorous editorial in the *Perth Courier* said, "Having the batteries charged is an annoyance but blessed is the motorist who has found a place to have gasoline charged." Other humour of the day is very similar to modern wishes. A prospective buyer walked into a garage in 1920 and said," I would like to see a first class second hand car." The proprietor looked at him, smiled, and said, "So would I, brother."

Late nights, young daughters and parental concerns are not issues of modern times only. In 1922, a worried parent put his family's new car to good use on a moonless night. With a lantern hung on the radiator cap, Jack Taylor drove slowly along the stony road toward a neighbouring farmhouse where his fun-loving daughters were at a dance. He met the high-spirited girls on the road and they ran to meet his welcome light, glad of a lift home so they no longer had to stumble over the ruts and ridges of the road.

Car troubles – they began as soon as automobile tires hit roads. One day a Galbraith farmer had gas pedal trouble and the vehicle needed to be taken to a garage. Archie Barr was asked to perform a delicate operation to help. His task was to pour gas slowly on the carburetor whilst perched on the hood of the car over the miles to town! The operation was successful and that ride as a hood ornament was not one soon forgotten.

Hearty laughs were shared for years about the trials of a young man who had more experience driving horses than newfangled automobiles. Morris Turner started home after a day at the Middleville Fair, proudly driving his 490 Chev Touring car. The hills proved too much for his skills with the brake and clutch and he ripped the gears out of the car. He had to leave the wrecked machine by the roadside. Later, he returned with a team of horses to pull the car home. A passing neighbour inquired as to the trouble and he answered with the wisecrack, "I ripped my rear end out."

Gas price wars and price gouging started in the early years of the operation of motorized vehicles. Gasoline supply stations and automobile trade representatives petitioned the federal government in 1918 to license the gasoline trade and to fix the margin of profit at twenty percent.[5]

Ways to save gasoline were popular lists to clip out and tack on the carriage shed cum garage doors along with stallion route bills, odd horseshoes and old snaps and buckles. Some of the suggestions included;

Avoid high speeds.
Stop gasoline leaks.
Don't accelerate quickly.
Stop engine and coast down hills.

Farm journals gave driving tips and also advocated the standardization of truck, car and wagon track widths. The width from tire to tire was narrower than the distance between wagon wheels. This meant that the wagon wheels went in the track on one side and up on the ridge on the other, causing discomfort for the teamsters and destablizing the loads on the wagons.

Highway Don'ts were favourite topics in newspapers in the early days of cars:

Don't blow your horn in an attempt to hurry a herd of cows off the road. It can't be done.

Don't start a race with a friend on a public highway.

Don't go back onto a main highway or away from the curb without holding your signal arm out.

Don't cut corners even in the country.

Don't depend on the other fellow to stop.

Carleton Place Herald, April, 1920.

An International Harvester advertisement in the *Family Herald* in 1925 riding the crest of the wave to supplant horses with mechanized power.

Motor cars had come to stay and old fashioned gravel roads or macadamized surfaces could not stand the strain of the new traffic. Governments, municipal and provincial, realized that well-maintained roads were essential to the farmers for transporting farm produce to markets and train stations. In 1920 motor licence fees were raised to pay for a highway improvement scheme. The fee for light cars of twenty-five horsepower, which included nearly all the moderately priced cars on the roadways, was raised three dollars to thirteen dollars.

By 1920 farm auction announcements listed, a "Ford car with good tires" or "Ford car in 1st class order," along with the wiffletrees, neck yokes, walking ploughs, double buggies, lumber wagons, goat robes, cutters and sets of sloops. Other signs of the changing times were garage ads that proudly announced that they were in a position to repair all makes of cars on short notice, as well as retaining their fine harness departments on the premises to do all kinds of repairs and to take orders for new custom-made harness.

For many years, winter travel remained the province of live horsepower. *Almonte Gazette* front page news in February, 1938 reported, "Roads in Great Shape. Teamsters agree that at the present time there is 'good going' on the roads with an icy bottom covered with a light layer of snow. Heavy loads can be handled without difficulty. The downhill grades present the only trouble and some have to resort to putting chains on the sleigh runners to slow up the descent."

In 1920, with automobiles becoming the fashion, harness makers advertised their products for heavy horses still used in farm work. PERTH COURIER, 1920

Seeing the writing on the wall livery stable owners bowed to market pressures and gradually their businesses were phased out. LANARK ERA, 1918

County road officials were torn between the demands of farmers driving sleighs, not to sand the roads, and the demands of motorists that the roads be sanded. The *Almonte Gazette* reported, "The plan of sanding a strip in the middle for wheeling and leaving unsanded stretches along each side for sleighs has been tried but it is said that the sand soon spreads over the entire width of the highway."

Long before automobiles were in use, wagon and buggy wheels churned dust into the air and calls for the watering of town streets were made. In the summer months, flying dust and grit caused annoyance to merchants as well as those who walked along streets and roadways. Dust sifted into stores and damaged the wares. Town councils heard insistent complaints as automobile traffic increased. Excessive dust in Smiths Falls resulted in the passing of a bylaw to oil the dusty streets.[6] Townspeople congratulated the town council for the decision.

The people of Almonte found the streets too dusty as well and appreciated the services of a water wagon. The newspaper reported in 1910, "After considerable delay the water wagon was put on its rounds this week. It was welcome. Greatly as we love our Dominion of Canada, very few of us want to eat it." Editorial comments in the *Lanark Era* of June, 1926 hoped "that automobile owners took baths oftener than their vehicles got them - to judge from the traffic passing outside his window."

Horsedrawn vehicles with no lights were in jeopardy from cars at night. Automobile drivers were incensed by the fact that no law compelled buggies or sleighs to have a lighted lantern or some other signal on their vehicles. Horsemen were encouraged not to wait for regulations to be passed, but to be a law unto themselves and light up their vehicles.

By 1927, an amendment to the Highways Traffic Act decreed that lights be placed on all vehicles driven by any kind of power including muscular power[7]. This clearly included vehicles drawn by horses or any other animal. However, as late as 1945, there was an accident reported that involved a car and an unlighted buggy travelling on a main road. Horses involved in terrifying accidents, even if they were unhurt in the pile-up, were of little use afterwards on roads with cars.

Speeding became a concern for county constables. A spiked plank speed trap was devised to deter speeders. It was a board studded with nails which was thrown on the road in front of a moving vehicle. The distance it would take for a driver travelling the speed limit or less was carefully marked off ahead of time. If the driver was able to stop in time to avoid the plank it meant the car was not speeding. If the tires hit the plank, the driver got a speeding ticket as well as a flat tire or two.[8]

Reports of automobile accidents began to make the news almost as soon as cars were on the roads. Young men were especially susceptible to the speed and power of the new machines. Mixed with alcohol, the results were often deadly. One evening after a few pulls at the bottle, a young man was riding on the running board of a chum's Model A Ford. The car lurched into a pot hole and the fellow was thrown off and fatally injured when he hit a telegraph pole. Local community news also reported the incidents where people had the misfortune to break an arm or strike a kneecap while cranking a car to start it.

> These Lost and Found advertisements tell the tale of the passage of time and the march of progress.
>
> LOST FROM PASTURE – One fox coloured mare. 1829
>
> LOST ON THE ROAD – A buffalo robe lined with carpet. Reward. 1887
>
> DOG FOUND – A brown spaniel with short tail followed my rig from near Carleton Place on July 17. Owner can have same by paying expenses. 1900
>
> LOST – A door handle from a car. Would finder please leave at or notify the newspaper office. 1935

The motor car was here to stay and pleas were made for drivers, as well as pedestrians, to be aware that cars were heavy, powerful machines. Drivers were warned to be ever mindful of their speed and of others on the roads. After a smash, it was of little advantage to drivers to know that they had had the right of way.

As the years passed there was room enough for all and the teamsters and chauffeurs cooperated on the sharing of the roadways. However, inexorably horsepower was replaced by motorized power and the pace of life changed forever. A new chapter of history unfolded on the roads.

---

1 Charles Philip Fox, *Horses In Harness*, (Reiman Associates, 1987), p.8.
2 Jean Rankin, Scrapbook, Courtesy of the Middleville and District Museum.
3 *The Power Age*, Ford Motor Advertising Circular, 1920.
4 *The Power Age*, 1920.
5 The *Rideau Record*, November, 1918.
6 The *Rideau Record*, May, 1918.
7 The *Lanark Era*, 1927.
8 Hazel Murphy, Rob Rivington, Tom VanAlstine, Sherry Tysik-Paul, *The Heritage Transportation Project, Phase 1*, Lanark Tourism Association, March, 1995, p. 19

Postscript

AS I HAVE ranged about in my imagination, recreating the traffic on the early, potted, country roadways, I see the paved road that passes my old farmhouse as a direct link with that past. Where once sleigh loads of cord wood screeched on the snowy road, now log trucks roar by at great speed. Where once wagons of milk cans rattled to the cheese factory, now shining, silver, bulk milk trucks gear down onto the side road, to collect milk from neighbouring farms. Voices once came over the hill as children made their way to the one-room schoolhouse. Now, a big yellow school bus stops along the road and as the children take their seats, it growls off with a blast of diesel fumes.

From the earliest rough paths through dark, dense forests to the paved roads of today, the highways and byways were the economic and social life lines of the countryside. Over the years of settlement, the action and drama on the roads of Lanark County was like a moving stage. It was a theatre with plot, colour and a cast of characters set against a backdrop of changing landscapes and changing times. Gypsies, tramps, pedlars and travelling preachers as well as lambs scampering along the road to market or sleighs piled high with frozen chickens and turkeys, headed for poultry fairs, have become things of memory only.

ACCT. 11103 #22. COURTESY OF THE MIDDLEVILLE AND DISTRICT MUSEUM

BIBLIOGRAPHY

The Beaver, Magazine Of The North, Spring,1966.

Bennett, Carol and D.W. McCuaig. *In Search of Lanark*, (Renfrew Advance Ltd., 1980).

Bond, C.C.J. "The Hudson's Bay Company in the Ottawa Valley."

Brown, Howard Morton. *Lanark Legacy Nineteenth Century Glimpses of An Ontario County*, (The Corporation Of The County of Lanark,1984).

Collins, John M. *The McIntosh Family Of Lanark County, Ontario*, (Second Edition,1991).

de Bairacli Levy, Juliette. *Herbal Handbook for Farm and Stable*, (Rodale Press Inc.1976).

Easton, George. 1830-1839 Diary, Courtesy of the Middleville Museum.

Enne, Dee Mac. (Donald McNicol), Courtesy of the Watson's Corners Museum.

Forbes, C.M. History of Lanark Covering an Eighty Five Year Period, *Perth Courier*, January, 1906.

Fox, Charles Phillip. *Horses In Harness*, (Reiman Associates, 1987).

Geddes, Hilda. *The Canadian Mississippi River*, (OmnigraphInc.1988).

Guillet, Edwin C. *The Pioneer And Backwoodsman*,Volume 1, (The Ontario Publishing Co. Ltd. 1963).

______. *The Story Of Canadian Roads*, (University of Toronto Press,1966).

______. & Jessie E. McEwen. *Finding New Homes In Canada*, (Thomas Nelson & Sons Ltd.), 1938.

Historical Sketch of McDonald's Corners, Snow Road and Elphin,1875-1995.

Kemp Affleck, Mrs. Eva. Scrapbook, Courtesy of the Middleville and District Museum.

Kirkland, Hal. The Aristocratic Bairds of Bennie's Corners, *Almonte Gazette*, undated in a scrapbook of Mrs. J.R. Reid's, Courtesy of the Middleville and District Museum.

Lalond, Robert. *A Narrative of the Rise and Progress of Emigration from the Counties of Lanark and Renfrew to the New Settlements of Upper Canada*; (Glasgow,1821), Canadian Heritage Publications,1978.

Lanark Township Records, 1853, 1858, 1859, 1865, 1871.

Lowry, Edna G. *A Family Record of Pioneer Scottish Families in Lanark County and Their Descendents.*

McIlraith, Penny. *A McIlraith History, Decendants of James McIlraith 1789-1881* (Toronto: Ontario, Canada,1985).

McKay, Mrs. Milton. Diary, 1925.

McNicol Family History, Courtesy of the Middleville and District Museum.

McNicol, Donald. *The Road To Perth*, Scrapbook, Mrs. J.R. Reid, Courtesy of the Middleville and District Museum.

Morgan H.P., Lieutenant J.C. *The Emigrant's Notebook and Guide with Recollections of Upper and Lower Canada During the Late War*, (London, 1824).

Ontario. *The Municipal Manual For Upper Canada*, 1855, 1885.

_______. *The Revised Statutes of Ontario*, 1877, 1879.

Rankin, James. Account book, 1872, Courtesy of the Middleville and District Museum.

Rankin, Jean. Scrapbook, Courtesy of the Middleville and District Museum.

Reid, Mrs. J.R. Scrapbook, Courtesy of the Middleville and District Museum.

Scadding, Henry. "The Astrolabes of Samuel Champlain and Geoffrey Chaucer,"*Rose Belford's Canadian Monthly and National Review*, Volume 5, Number 6, (December,1880).

Smith, William Wye. "Illustrations of Canadian Life,"*Rose Belford's Canadian Monthly and National Review*, Vol.8, No.3 (March 1882).

_______. *New Dominion Monthly*, 1882, Vol. 8, No.2.

Talbot, Edward Allen. *Five Years Residence in the Canadas including a Tour Through Part of the United States of America in the Year 1823*; (Longman, Hurst, Rees, Orme, Brown and Green, London, 1824).

Tennant, Joseph. Diary, 1887.

Tennant, Robert D. *Geneology of the Tennant Family*, 1963.

The American Agriculturalist, November, 1881.

Whitton, Charlotte. *A Hundred Years A-Fellin" 1842-1924*, (Gillies Brothers, Limited, Braeside, Ontario, 1943).

Biographical Note

The history of Lanark County has been a passionate interest for Claudia Smith, ever since she moved to her farm near Almonte with her husband in 1980. She is a history columnist for the *Lanark Era*, a gatherer of oral history and a photographer of artifacts and rural relics of times past. Chance comments about gypsies put her on the trail of the colourful history of Lanark County's roads.

Claudia combines her interest in history and community with volunteer work at the Middleville and District Museum and the Middleville Agricultural Society. This second book follows *When the Sugar Bird Sings, The History of Maple Syrup in Lanark County* (General Store Publishing House).